DATE			

Messages

Messages

A Thematic Anthology of Poetry

Edited by X. J. Kennedy Tufts University

Little, Brown and Company

Boston

Library of Congress Catalog Card Number: 72-9907

First Printing

Published simultaneously in Canada
by Little, Brown & Company (Canada) Limited

Printed in the United States of America

Photo Credits
P.   2. Larry Keenan, Jr., Photofind, S.F.
P.   22. William Klein
P.   50. Hiroshi Hamaya, Magnum
P.   84. Silver Images, Black Star
P. 114. Harry Callahan
P. 138. Copyright by W. Eugene Smith
P. 162. Copyright by H. W. Silvester, Rapho-Guillumette
P. 194. Roland Patterson, Black Star
P. 216. Copyright by Larry Keenan, Jr., Photofind, S.F.
P. 252. Larry Keenan, Jr., Photofind, S.F.
P. 276. Ernest Lowe, Photofind, S.F.
P. 304. Lawrence Cameron

Copyrights and Acknowledgments
The author is grateful to the following publishers and copyright holders for permission to use the poetry reprinted in this book.

ABC Contemporary Music Publishing. "Why I Sing the Blues" by B. B. King, copyright © 1969 by Pamco Music, Inc., 8255 Beverly Blvd., Los Angeles, Calif. 90048. All rights reserved. Used by permission.
Helen Adam. "The House o' the Mirror," first published by the Acadia Press, is reprinted by permission of the poet.
American Folklore Society. "The Two Sisters" is reprinted by permission of the American Folklore Society, Inc.
Atheneum Publishers. "The Roof Garden" from Selected Poems by Howard Moss, copyright © 1965, 1971 by Howard Moss. "The Blue Whale" from Advantages of Dark by Robert Watson, copyright © 1966 by Robert Watson. "They Feed They Lion" from They Feed They Lion by Philip Levine, copyright © 1972 by Philip Levine. "Eating Poetry" from Reasons for Moving by Mark Strand, copyright © 1966 by Mark Strand; first appeared in The New York Review of Books. "The Dover Bitch" from The Hard Hours by Anthony Hecht, copyright © 1960 by Anthony Hecht; first appeared in Transatlantic Review. "Hands" from A Joyful Noise by Donald Finkel, copyright © 1965, 1966 by Donald Finkel. "Laboratory

viii

Preface

In a dark time, the eye begins to see . . .
THEODORE ROETHKE

My assumption in this book is that poetry — whatever its many
pleasures — has something to say to people. In the first half of
the anthology, after an opening section of poems about poetry
itself (in which, I hope, some of those pleasures will be
suggested), there are almost a hundred poems on subjects of
present-day urgency. Some of these concerns, it will appear,
are not new to poetry. Because my intention is to offer
rewarding poems without caring whether their authors are
unknown or famous, many selections have been taken from
recent books and little magazines; but familiar works by major
poets of the past also have been included. The reader must
decide whether the older poems have any immediate truth
or whether, as Carl Sandburg put it, the past is a bucket of ashes.
So that the reader may make his decision without being
distracted from the poetry itself, the poets' by-lines do not
appear with their poems; instead, the names of the poets are
given at the end of the book.

My belief is that certain older and unfashionable poems,
given a sympathetic hearing, will be found to contain much
that is pertinent. Although in his lifetime Emerson did not
face the threat of ecological disaster, nevertheless he was keenly
aware of the fragile hospitality the earth extends to men. To
read his "Hamatreya" together with a recent poem (also
indebted to Eastern holy scriptures) on a similar theme, the
anonymous "Smokey the Bear Sutra," may make us sense a few
fresh relationships. It is well to beware of easy identifications
of the "relevant" with the contemporary. At the same time,
it is well to beware of facile assumptions that Shakespeare's
concerns and our own are identical. History never completely
repeats itself. At times, juxtapositions of new and old poems
may suggest contrasts. Does Sir Philip Sidney's sonnet to the
moon, for instance, express attitudes still possible for us in the
1970's, now that (as contemporary poets John Engels and
William Meredith reveal) men have walked on the moon as

though it were conquered territory? At the very least, I hope this book will provide occasions for good argument.

In the latter half, the poems may remind us of human satisfactions, motifs long alive in men's imaginations (journeys, magic), alternatives to our self-destruction. I have tried to avoid expressions of smug optimism and smug despair and to favor poems that express hope with hard-eyed caution. The arrangement of poems in categories is inevitably arbitrary, and the reader may find many that can fit just as well into one category as into another. There is an order to the arrangement of poems in each thematic section, but it varies from one section to another. In general, I have tried to set poems side by side or in groupings where they may best throw light on one another.

One danger inherent in the thematic approach to poetry is to want to read poetry for its subject matter, for what can be paraphrased, without regard for the special qualities of language and imagination that are, after all, what distinguish poems from prose. Gerard Manley Hopkins reminds us, in a famous definition, that poetry may be seen as "speech framed . . . to be heard for its own sake and interest even over and above its interest of meaning." W. H. Auden has warned that poets who wish to change the world (but who aren't especially interested in trivial things such as words) tend to be unreadable. Aware of the perils of *mere* message-making, Ezra Pound has affirmed that in poetry only emotion endures. True enough, and yet is it not also true that strong language and strong emotion in poetry often arise out of strong convictions? Many enduring lyrics have been the work of poets deeply committed to causes — Milton, Blake, and Yeats, to name a few — poets passionately troubled and concerned for man's commonweal. If we still care to read their expressions of concern, it may be because they were first of all poets, not polemicists. But the best poets often show us some truth we hadn't realized before, even when (it would seem) they write for the pleasure of putting words together.

A difficulty in compiling this book was the current abundance of poems on topics of great immediacy that appear on reflection to be indifferent poetry. To read very much contemporary poetry is soon to be aware that many poetic statements on war, injustice, and the troubles of our cities — however admirable they may be as statements — remain dull honest thoughts in forgettable words; they seem less pertinent than do some traditional folk ballads of the Middle Ages. In the end, my main criterion for including poems was the conviction that a poem, through the power of its language and imagination, had been an experience that had remained with me. It would be too much to expect the reader's taste always to parallel mine: "One man's meat," goes a saying, "is another man's anthology." However, at least some of these poems may anger, offend, astonish, challenge, and regale. Some of them may even offer peace — or the possibility of it. That is what good poetry has always done. We can only trust that it will continue to do so always.

I want to thank Dorothy M. Kennedy for reading and criticizing this book in manuscript; Tom Sears and David Zolotow for offering early encouragement; Gibson M. Leonard of the Committee for Aid to Schools for helping to define my project; Barbara Levitt for discovering the photographs; Henry Taylor, Sylvan Barnet, David Giele, Maggie Rennert, and Frank Graham for giving advice and counsel; Charles H. Christensen and Pat Herbst for creative editing; and John Michael Brennan and other former students at Tufts for ripping apart my first-planned table of contents and helping me perhaps to see a little more clearly into their aspirations.

Contents

Messages

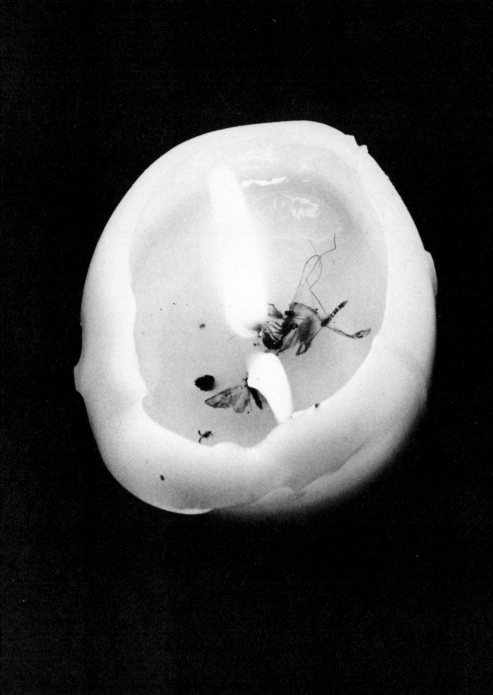

1. By Singing Light

The Nature of Poetry

In my craft or sullen art

In my craft or sullen art
Exercised in the still night
When only the moon rages
And the lovers lie abed
With all their griefs in their arms,
I labor by singing light
Not for ambition or bread
Or the strut and the trade of charms
On the ivory stages
But for the common wages
Of their most secret heart.

Not for the proud man apart
From the raging moon I write
On these spindrift pages
Nor for the towering dead
With their nightingales and psalms
But for the lovers, their arms
Round the griefs of the ages,
Who pay no praise or wages
Nor heed my craft or art.

A Fit of Rime Against Rime

Rime, the rack of finest wits,
That expresseth but by fits
    True conceit,
Spoiling senses of their treasure,
Cozening judgment with a measure,
    But false weight;
Wresting words from their true calling,
Propping verse for fear of falling
    To the ground;
Jointing syllables, drowning letters,
Fast'ning vowels as with fetters
    They were bound!
Soon as lazy thou wert known,
All good poetry hence was flown,
    And art banished.
For a thousand years together
All Parnassus' green did wither
    And wit vanished.
Pegasus did fly away,
At the well no Muse did stay,
    But bewailed
So to see the fountain dry
And Apollo's music die,
    All light failed!
Starveling rimes did fill the stage;
Not a poet in an age
    Worth a crowning;
Not a work deserving bays,
Nor a line deserving praise,
    Pallas frowning;
Greek was free from rime's infection,
Happy Greek by this protection
    Was not spoiled.
Whilst the Latin, queen of tongues,
Is not yet free from rime's wrongs,
    But rests foiled.
Scarce the hill again doth flourish,

Scarce the world a wit doth nourish
          To restore
40 Phoebus to his crown again,
And the Muses to their brain,
          As before.
Vulgar languages that want
Words and sweetness, and be scant
45   Of true measure,
Tyrant rhyme hath so abused
That they long since have refused
          Other caesure.
He that first invented thee,
50 May his joints tormented be,
          Cramped forever.
Still may syllables jar with time,
Still may reason war with rime,
          Resting never.
55 May his sense when it would meet
The cold tumor in his feet
          Grow unsounder;
And his title be long fool
That in rearing such a school
60   Was the founder.

3 *conceit:* poetic imagination.   5 *cozening:* deceiving.   17 *Parnassus:* in
Greek and Roman mythology, the mountain of Apollo, god of music
and poetry.   19 *Pegasus:* poetic inspiration. Legend has it that the winged
horse Pegasus stamped the ground, causing the fountain of the Muses
to burst forth.   37 *hill:* Parnassus.   40 *Phoebus:* Apollo.   48 *caesure:* or
cesura, a pause in a line of poetry.

7

Letter to a Librarian

Mr. P. — I have heard it rumored
That you, humanist, librarian with a license,
In the shady privacy of your glassed room
Tore up my book of poems.

Sir, a word in your ear. Others
Have tried that game: burned Mann
And my immortal kinsman Heine.
Idiots! What act could be vainer?

For this act of yours, the ligatures
Pest-corroded, your eyes shall fall
From their sockets; drop on your lacquered desk
With the dull weight of pinballs.

And brighter than the sapless vine
Your hands shall flare;
To the murkiest kimbos of the library
Flashing my name like a neon sign.

And the candid great
Of whom not one was ever an Australian
Cry dustily from their shelves,
"Imposter! False custodian!"

Till a stunned derelict
You fall down blind, ear-beleaguered,
While Rabelais pipes you a wished-for death
On a kazoo quaint and silvered.

Eating Poetry

Ink runs from the corners of my mouth.
There is no happiness like mine.
I have been eating poetry.

The librarian does not believe what she sees.
Her eyes are sad
and she walks with her hands in her dress.

The poems are gone.
The light is dim.
The dogs are on the basement stairs and coming up.

Their eyeballs roll,
their blond legs burn like brush.
The poor librarian begins to stamp her feet and weep.

She does not understand.
When I get on my knees and lick her hand,
she screams.

I am a new man.
I snarl at her and bark.
I romp with joy in the bookish dark.

Throughout the world, if it were sought

Throughout the world, if it were sought,
Fair words enough a man shall find:
They be good cheap, they cost right nought,
Their substance is but only wind;
   But well to say and so to mean,
   That sweet accord is seldom seen.

The Muse

The Muse came pulling off her gown
and nine feet tall she laid her down
and I by her side a popinjay
with nothing to say. Did she mean to stay?

She smelled like flame, like starch on sweat,
like sperm; like shame; like a launderette.
No one, she said, *has loved me right.*
Day and night. Day and night.

Dover Beach

The sea is calm tonight.
The tide is full, the moon lies fair
Upon the straits; on the French coast the light
Gleams and is gone; the cliffs of England stand,
Glimmering and vast, out in the tranquil bay.
Come to the window, sweet is the night air!
Only, from the long line of spray
Where the sea meets the moon-blanched land,
Listen! you hear the grating roar
Of pebbles which the waves draw back, and fling,
At their return, up the high strand,
Begin, and cease, and then again begin,
With tremulous cadence slow, and bring
The eternal note of sadness in.

Sophocles long ago
Heard it on the Ægean, and it brought
Into his mind the turbid ebb and flow
Of human misery; we
Find also in the sound a thought,
Hearing it by this distant northern sea.

The Sea of Faith
Was once, too, at the full, and round earth's shore
Lay like the folds of a bright girdle furled.
But now I only hear
Its melancholy, long, withdrawing roar,
Retreating, to the breath
Of the night wind, down the vast edges drear
And naked shingles of the world.

Ah, love, let us be true
30   To one another! for the world, which seems
To lie before us like a land of dreams,
So various, so beautiful, so new,
Hath really neither joy, nor love, nor light,
Nor certitude, nor peace, nor help for pain;
35   And we are here as on a darkling plain,
Swept with confused alarms of struggle and flight,
Where ignorant armies clash by night.

28 *shingles*: gravel beaches.   35 *darkling*: darkened or darkening.

13

The Dover Bitch
A Criticism of Life

For Andrews Wanning

So there stood Matthew Arnold and this girl
With the cliffs of England crumbling away behind them,
And he said to her, "Try to be true to me,
And I'll do the same for you, for things are bad
All over, etc., etc."
Well now, I knew this girl. It's true she had read
Sophocles in a fairly good translation
And caught that bitter allusion to the sea,
But all the time he was talking she had in mind
The notion of what his whiskers would feel like
On the back of her neck. She told me later on
That after a while she got to looking out
At the lights across the channel, and really felt sad,
Thinking of all the wine and enormous beds
And blandishments in French and the perfumes.
And then she got really angry. To have been brought
All the way down from London, and then be addressed
As a sort of mournful cosmic last resort
Is really tough on a girl, and she was pretty.
Anyway, she watched him pace the room
And finger his watch-chain and seem to sweat a bit,
And then she said one or two unprintable things.
But you mustn't judge her by that. What I mean to say is,
She's really all right. I still see her once in a while
And she always treats me right. We have a drink
And I give her a good time, and perhaps it's a year
Before I see her again, but there she is,
Running to fat, but dependable as they come.
And sometimes I bring her a bottle of *Nuit d'Amour*.

crickets

crickets
crickets
crickets
crickets
crickets
crickets
crickets
crickets
crickets
crickets
crickets
crickets
crickets
crickets
crickets
crickets
crickets
crickets
crickets
crickets
crickets
crickets
crickets
crickets
crickets
crickets
crickets
crickets
crickets
crickets
crickets
crickets
crickets
crickets
crickets
crickets

Spring and Fall

To a Young Child

Márgarét, are you gríeving
Over Goldengrove unleaving?
Leáves, like the things of man, you
With your fresh thoughts care for, can you?
Ah! ás the heart grows older
It will come to such sights colder
By and by, nor spare a sigh
Though worlds of wanwood leafmeal lie;
And yet you wíll weep and know why.
Now no matter, child, the name:
Sórrow's spríngs áre the same.
Nor mouth had, no nor mind, expressed
What heart heard of, ghost guessed:
It ís the blight man was born for,
It is Margaret you mourn for.

2 *unleaving:* shedding its leaves.   13 *ghost:* spirit.

16

Margaret Are You Drug

Cool it Mag.
Sure it's a drag
With all that green flaked out.
Next thing you know they'll be changing the color of bread.

5 But look, Chick,
Why panic?
Sevennyeighty years, we'll *all* be dead.

Roll with it, Kid.
I did.
10 Give it the old benefit of the doubt.

I mean leaves
Schmeaves.
You sure you aint just feeling sorry for yourself?

This is one of a series of "Translations from the English."

Hands

The poem makes truth a little more disturbing,
like a good bra, lifts it and holds it out
in both hands. (In some of the flashier stores
there's a model with the hands stitched on, in red or black.)

5 Lately the world you wed, for want of such hands,
sags in the bed beside you like a tired wife.
For want of such hands, the face of the moon is bored,
the tree does not stretch and yearn, nor the groin tighten.

Devious or frank, in any case,
10 the poem is calculated to arouse.
Lean back and let its hands play freely on you:
there comes a moment, lifted and aroused,
when the two of you are equally beautiful.

And did those feet in ancient time

And did those feet in ancient time
    Walk upon England's mountains green?
And was the holy Lamb of God
    On England's pleasant pastures seen?

5   And did the Countenance Divine
    Shine forth upon our clouded hills?
And was Jerusalem builded here
    Among these dark Satanic mills?

Bring me my bow of burning gold!
10   Bring me my arrows of desire!
Bring me my spear! O clouds, unfold!
    Bring me my chariot of fire!

I will not cease from mental fight,
    Nor shall my sword sleep in my hand,
15   Till we have built Jerusalem
    In England's green and pleasant land.

Blake placed these lines at the end of the preface to "Milton," a prophetic poem in which he calls for a poetry based on sheer inspiration and imagination rather than on classical models.

The Circus Animals' Desertion

I

I sought a theme and sought for it in vain,
I sought it daily for six weeks or so.
Maybe at last, being but a broken man,
I must be satisfied with my heart, although
Winter and summer till old age began
My circus animals were all on show,
Those stilted boys, that burnished chariot,
Lion and woman and the Lord knows what.

II

What can I but enumerate old themes?
First that sea-rider Oisin led by the nose
Through three enchanted islands, allegorical dreams,
Vain gaiety, vain battle, vain repose,
Themes of the embittered heart, or so it seems,
That might adorn old songs or courtly shows;
But what cared I that set him on to ride,
I, starved for the bosom of his faery bride?

And then a counter-truth filled out its play,
The Countess Cathleen was the name I gave it;
She, pity-crazed, had given her soul away,
But masterful Heaven had intervened to save it.
I thought my dear must her own soul destroy,
So did fanaticism and hate enslave it,
And this brought forth a dream and soon enough
This dream itself had all my thought and love.

And when the Fool and Blind Man stole the bread
Cuchulain fought the ungovernable sea;
Heart-mysteries there, and yet when all is said
It was the dream itself enchanted me:
Character isolated by a deed
To engross the present and dominate memory.
Players and painted stage took all my love,
And not those things that they were emblems of.

III

Those masterful images because complete
Grew in pure mind, but out of what began?
A mound of refuse or the sweepings of a street,
Old kettles, old bottles, and a broken can,
Old iron, old bones, old rags, that raving slut
Who keeps the till. Now that my ladder's gone,
I must lie down where all the ladders start,
In the foul rag-and-bone shop of the heart.

35

40

By circus animals Yeats means the images, symbols, and motifs employed
in his earlier poetry.   10 *sea-rider Oisin:* In his long poem *The
Wanderings of Oisin* (1889), Yeats tells of voyages to three fantastic
islands undertaken by Oisin (pronounced *Usheen*), a legendary hero and
poet.   18 *The Countess Cathleen:* Yeats's first play (1892), about a
noblewoman who bargains with demons during a famine: her soul in
exchange for food to give to starving peasants.   21 *my dear:* Maud Gonne,
whom Yeats had long courted unsuccessfully. She had acted the title role
in *The Countess Cathleen.* Yeats disapproved of what he considered her
excessive zeal in the cause of Irish independence.   25–26 *Fool and Blind
Man . . . Cuchulain:* In Yeats's play *On Baile's Strand* (1904), fool and blind
man are characters who steal for a living. In the same play King Cuchulain
(pronounced *CuHOOLan)* dies in a frenzy, flailing at the waves with
his sword.

2. Marks of Woe

Cities

London

I wander through each chartered street,
Near where the chartered Thames does flow,
And mark in every face I meet
Marks of weakness, marks of woe.

5 In every cry of every man,
In every infant's cry of fear,
In every voice, in every ban,
The mind-forged manacles I hear.

How the chimney-sweeper's cry
10 Every black'ning church appalls;
And the hapless soldier's sigh
Runs in blood down palace walls.

But most through midnight streets I hear
How the youthful harlot's curse
15 Blasts the new-born infant's tear,
And blights with plagues the marriage hearse.

A Documentary on Airplane Glue

I have seen the young Negroes & Puerto Ricans
sniffing and nodding in their slums
the young ones
old enough to afford only
5   the 25-cent Carbona or airplane glue
        the glue so paradoxically manufactured
for the assemblage of model airplanes/

I see the young boys 10   11   13 years
drawing nostrils to bottle lip
10   and then staring woozily at their tenements
twice & thrice as old as their parents
or gazing at the monotonous pink dormitories
of the Housing Authority
set up so their fathers can remain at their meager jobs
15   or their mothers on relief/

The pink buildings are tall
the tiny balsa wood planes the glue holds so well
never fly
        try to fly them & they'll break
20   leave them lying around & they'll be broken
most of these boys
      have never been on a real plane
           and never will
           (unless they return to Puerto Rico
25   flying from poverty to poverty above the clouds/
      . . . & *not* back to Africa)

& for a moment at least   sniffing the glue

can soar one above the pink & gray buildings/

the balsa wood planes are delicate
30   and crush easily
           Sometimes I wonder how the effects
           of the glue was discovered?

Could it have been an eleven-year-old
bending so close to the tiny construction
35   piecing & glueing & piecing
gasping with slight exasperation
& then suddenly   wonderfully
                              soaring
              ultimately away/

On Seeing a Torn Out Coin Telephone

Way to call up quick wishes —
Pizza or chicken — black disaster
Lies there so no one can report
Terror — to try the police once more.

5   The first thing stupidity says
Rather than face that hollow cell —
Saturday Night at the Movies — hits
My mind, "Get me a mouthpiece."

                            Wait:

The crazy bell of a drunk laugh.
10   Instrument, whose nails call for help?
At what man shall I point? Attila
Bludgeons Orion down — while

Civilization, a word too big
For a ten cent call, lies there mute,
15   Silenced dummy — and who will know
Tonight how many die alone.

In Montecito

In a fashionable suburb of Santa Barbara,
Montecito, there visited me one night at midnight
A scream with breasts. As it hung there in the sweet air
That was always the right temperature, the contractors
Who had undertaken to dismantle it, stripped off
The lips, let the air out of the breasts.
                         People disappear
Even in Montecito. Greenie Taliaferro,
In her white maillot, her good figure almost firm,
Her old pepper-and-salt hair stripped by the hairdresser
To nothing and dyed platinum — Greenie has left her Bentley.
They have thrown away her electric toothbrush, someone else
    slips
The key into the lock of her safety-deposit box
At the Crocker-Anglo Bank; her seat at the cricket matches
Is warmed by buttocks less delectable than hers.
Greenie's girdle is empty.
                      A scream hangs there in the night:
They strip off the lips, let the air out of the breasts,
And Greenie has gone into the Greater Montecito
That surrounds Montecito like the echo of a scream.

The Roof Garden

A nervous hose is dribbling on the tar
This morning on this rooftop where I'm watching you
Move among your sparse, pinchpenny flowers,
Poor metronomes of color one month long
5 That pull the sun's rays in as best they can
And suck life up from one mere inch of dirt.
There's water in the sky but it won't come down.

Once we counted the skyline's water towers,
Barrels made of shingle, fat and high,
10 An African village suspended above
The needle hardness of New York that needs
More light than God provides to make it soft,
That needs the water in the water towers
To snake through pipe past all the elevators
15 To open up in bowls and baths and showers.

Soon our silence will dissolve in talk,
In talk that needs some water and some sun,
Or it will go the same way as before:
Dry repetitions of the ill we bear
20 Each other, the baited poles of light
Angling through the way the sun today
Fishes among the clouds.

                              Now you are through
Watering geraniums, and now you go
To the roof edge to survey the real estate
25 Of architectured air — tense forms wrought up,
Torn down, replaced, to be torn down again . . .
So much like us. Your head against the sky
Is topped by a tower clock, blocks away,
Whose two black hands are closing on the hour,
30 And I look down into the street below,
Rinsed fresh this morning by a water truck,
Down which a girl, perky in high heels,
Clops by, serenely unaware of us,
Of the cables, gas lines, telephone wires,
35 And water mains, writhing underfoot.

30

Quiet Town

Here in our cloud we talk
baking powder. Our yeast feet
make tracks that fill up with fog.
Tongue like a sponge, we describe
the air that we eat — how it has its own
lungs, inhales many a stranger.

Our stories have executives who flash
ornamental knives. Their children use them
afternoons to toast marshmallows.
Technicians in suicide plan courses
in high school for as long as it takes.

For our gestures, feathers are emphatic
enough; a snowflake smashes through
revealed rock. Our town balances,
and we have a railroad. Pitiful bandits
who storm the bank are led away,
their dreamy guns kicked into the gutter
by kids coming out of the movie.

No one is allowed to cross our lake at night.
Every Christmas we forget by selective remembering.
Overhead planes mutter our fear
and are dangerous, are bombs exploding
a long time, carrying bombs elsewhere to explode.

31

Before a Cashier's Window
in a Department Store

1.

The beautiful cashier's white face has risen once more
Behind a young manager's shoulder.
They whisper together, and stare
Straight into my face.
I feel like grabbing a stray child
Or a skinny old woman
And driving into a cellar, crouching
Under a stone bridge, praying myself sick,
Till the troops pass.

2.

Why should he care? He goes.
I slump deeper.
In my frayed coat, I am pinned down
By debt. He nods,
Commending my flesh to the pity of the daws of God.

3.

Am I dead? And, if not, why not?
For she sails there, alone, looming in the heaven of the beautiful.
She knows
The bulldozers will scrape me up
After dark, behind
The officers' club.
Beneath her terrible blaze, my skeleton
Glitters out. I am the dark. I am the dark
Bone I was born to be.

4.

Tu Fu woke shuddering on a battlefield
Once, in the dead of night, and made out
The mangled women, sorting
The haggard slant-eyes.
The moon was up.

5.

I am hungry. In two more days
It will be spring. So this
Is what it feels like.

24 *Tu Fu:* one of the greatest Chinese poets (A.D. 712–770), some of
whose poems tell of his life during frontier wars and famines.

The Bean Eaters

They eat beans mostly, this old yellow pair.
Dinner is a casual affair.
Plain chipware on a plain and creaking wood,
Tin flatware.

Two who are Mostly Good.
Two who have lived their day,
But keep on putting on their clothes
And putting things away.

And remembering . . .
Remembering, with twinklings and twinges,
As they lean over the beans in their rented back room that is full
      of beads and receipts and dolls and cloths, tobacco crumbs,
      vases and fringes.

The Tunnel
from *The Bridge*

To Find the Western path
Right thro' the Gates of Wrath.
　　—BLAKE

Performances, assortments, résumés —
Up Times Square to Columbus Circle lights
Channel the congresses, nightly sessions,
Refractions of the thousand theatres, faces —
Mysterious kitchens. . . . You shall search them all.
Someday by heart you'll learn each famous sight
And watch the curtain lift in hell's despite;
You'll find the garden in the third act dead,
Finger your knees — and wish yourself in bed
With tabloid crime-sheets perched in easy sight.

　　　　Then let you reach your hat
　　　　and go.
　　　　As usual, let you — also
　　　　walking down — exclaim
　　　　to twelve upward leaving
　　　　a subscription praise
　　　　for what time slays.

Or can't you quite make up your mind to ride;
A walk is better underneath the L a brisk
Ten blocks or so before? But you find yourself
Preparing penguin flexions of the arms, —
As usual you will meet the scuttle yawn:
The subway yawns the quickest promise home.

Be minimum, then, to swim the hiving swarms
Out of the Square, the Circle burning bright —
Avoid the glass doors gyring at your right,
Where boxed alone a second, eyes take fright
— Quite unprepared rush naked back to light:
And down beside the turnstile press the coin
Into the slot. The gongs already rattle.

35

And so
of cities you bespeak
subways, rivered under streets
and rivers. . . . In the car
35   the overtone of motion
underground, the monotone
of motion is the sound
of other faces, also underground —

"Let's have a pencil Jimmy — living now
40   at Floral Park
Flatbush — on the fourth of July —
like a pigeon's muddy dream — potatoes
to dig in the field — travlin the town — too —
night after night — the Culver line — the
45   girls all shaping up — it used to be — "

Our tongues recant like beaten weather vanes.
This answer lives like verdigris, like hair
Beyond extinction, surcease of the bone;
And repetition freezes — "What

50   "what do you want? getting weak on the links?
fandaddle daddy don't ask for change — IS THIS
FOURTEENTH? it's half past six she said — if
you don't like my gate why did you
swing on it, why *didja*
55   swing on it
anyhow — "

        And somehow anyhow swing —

The phonographs of hades in the brain
Are tunnels that re-wind themselves, and love
60   A burnt match skating in a urinal —
Somewhere above Fourteenth TAKE THE EXPRESS
To brush some new presentiment of pain —

"But I want service in this office SERVICE
I said — after
65 the show she cried a little afterwards but — "

Whose head is swinging from the swollen strap?
Whose body smokes along the bitten rails,
Bursts from a smoldering bundle far behind
In back forks of the chasms of the brain, —
70 Puffs from a riven stump far out behind
In interborough fissures of the mind . . . ?

And why do I often meet your visage here,
Your eyes like agate lanterns — on and on
Below the toothpaste and the dandruff ads?
75 — And did their riding eyes right through your side,
And did their eyes like unwashed platters ride?
And Death, aloft, — gigantically down
Probing through you — toward me, O evermore!
And when they dragged your retching flesh,
80 Your trembling hands that night through Baltimore —
That last night on the ballot rounds, did you
Shaking, did you deny the ticket, Poe?

For Gravesend Manor change at Chambers Street.
The platform hurries along to a dead stop.

85 The intent escalator lifts a serenade
Stilly
Of shoes, umbrellas, each eye attending its shoe, then
Bolting outright somewhere above where streets
Burst suddenly in rain. . . . The gongs recur:
90 Elbows and levers, guard and hissing door.
Thunder is galvothermic here below. . . . The car
Wheels off. The train rounds, bending to a scream,
Taking the final level for the dive
Under the river —
95 And somewhat emptier than before,
Demented, for a hitching second, humps; then

37

Lets go. . . . Toward corners of the floor
Newspapers wing, revolve and wing.
Blank windows gargle signals through the roar.

100 And does the Dæmon take you home, also,
Wop washerwoman, with the bandaged hair?
After the corridors are swept, the cuspidors —
The gaunt sky-barracks cleanly now, and bare,
O Genoese, do you bring mother eyes and hands
105 Back home to children and to golden hair?

Dæmon, demurring and eventful yawn!
Whose hideous laughter is a bellows mirth
— Or the muffled slaughter of a day in birth —
O cruelly to inoculate the brinking dawn
110 With antennæ toward worlds that glow and sink; —
To spoon us out more liquid than the dim
Locution of the eldest star, and pack
The conscience navelled in the plunging wind,
Umbilical to call — and straightway die!

115 O caught like pennies beneath soot and steam,
Kiss of our agony thou gatherest;
Condensed, thou takest all — shrill ganglia
Impassioned with some song we fail to keep.
And yet, like Lazarus, to feel the slope,
120 The sod and billow breaking, — lifting ground,
— A sound of waters bending astride the sky
Unceasing with some Word that will not die . . . !

*

A tugboat, wheezing wreaths of steam,
Lunged past, with one galvanic blare stove up the River.
125 I counted the echoes assembling, one after one,
Searching, thumbing the midnight on the piers.
Lights, coasting, left the oily tympanum of waters;
The blackness somewhere gouged glass on a sky.
And this thy harbor, O my City, I have driven under,

38

130　Tossed from the coil of ticking towers. . . . Tomorrow,
　　　And to be. . . . Here by the River that is East —
　　　Here at the waters' edge the hands drop memory;
　　　Shadowless in that abyss they unaccounting lie.
　　　How far away the star has pooled the sea —
135　Or shall the hands be drawn away, to die?

　　　Kiss of our agony Thou gatherest,
　　　　　　　　　　O Hand of Fire
　　　　　　　　　　　　　　gatherest —

---

77 *And Death . . . down:* See Edgar Allan Poe's "The City in the Sea,"
page 184. 100 *the Dæmon:* here, the subway; perhaps also a personification
of the Machine.　119 *Lazarus:* whom Christ raised from the dead
(John 11 : 1–44).

dear mister congressman

dear mister congressman:
it's about my house — some time
ago i made a deal with a syrup company
to advertise their product on the side
facing the street — it wasnt so bad at
first, but soon they put up another
ad on the other side — i didn't even
mind that, but then they plastered
these women all over the windows with
cans of syrup in their arms — in exchange
the company paid my phone & gas bill &
bought a few clothes for the tots — i told
the town council that i'd do most anything
just to let some sun in the house but they
said we couldnt offend the syrup company
because it's called Granma Washington's
Syrup & people tend to associate it with
the constitution . . . the neighbors dont help
me at all because they feel that if anything
comes off my house, it'll have to go on theirs
& none of them want their houses looking like
mine — the company offered to buy my house as a
permanent billboard sign, but God, i got my
roots here & i had to refuse at first — now they
tell me some negroes are moving in down the
block — as you can see, things dont look
too good at the moment — my eldest son is
in the army so he cant do a thing — i
would appreciate any helpful suggestion —
thank you

                              yours in allegiance
                              Zorba the Bomb

40

National Cold Storage Company

The National Cold Storage Company contains
More things than you can dream of.
Hard by the Brooklyn Bridge it stands
In a litter of freight cars,
Tugs to one side; the other, the traffic
Of the Long Island Expressway.
I myself have dropped into it in seven years
Midnight tossings, plans for escape, the shakes.
Add this to the national total —
Grant's tomb, the Civil War, Arlington,
The young President dead.
Above the warehouse and beneath the stars
The poets creep on the harp of the Bridge.
But see,
They fall into the National Cold Storage Company
One by one. The wind off the river is too cold,
Or the times too rough, or the Bridge
Is not a harp at all. Or maybe
A monstrous birth inside the warehouse
Must be fed by everything — ships, poems,
Stars, all the years of our lives.

A Description of a City Shower

Careful observers may foretell the hour
(By sure prognostics) when to dread a shower:
While rain depends, the pensive cat gives o'er
Her frolics, and pursues her tail no more.
Returning home at night, you'll find the sink
Strike your offended sense with double stink.
If you be wise, then go not far to dine;
You'll spend in coach-hire more than save in wine.
A coming shower your shooting corns presage,
Old aches throb, your hollow tooth will rage.
Sauntering in coffeehouse is *Dulman* seen;
He damns the climate and complains of spleen.
    Meanwhile the South, rising with dabbled wings,
A sable cloud athwart the welkin flings,
That swilled more liquor than it could contain,
And like a drunkard gives it up again.
Brisk *Susan* whips her linen from the rope,
While the first drizzling shower is borne aslope:
Such is that sprinkling which some careless queen
Flirts on you from her mop, but not so clean:
You fly, invoke the gods; then turning, stop
To rail; she singing, still whirls on her mop.
Not yet the dust had shunned the unequal strife,
But, aided by the wind, fought still for life,
And wafted with its foe by violent gust,
'Twas doubtful which was rain and which was dust.
Ah! where must needy poet seek for aid,
When dust and rain at once his coat invade?
Sole coat, where dust cemented by the rain
Erects the nap, and leaves a mingled stain.
    Now in contiguous drops the flood comes down,
Threatening with deluge this devoted town.
To shops in crowds the daggled females fly,
Pretend to cheapen goods, but nothing buy.
The Templar spruce, while every spout's a-broach,
Stays till 'tis fair, yet seems to call a coach.

The tucked-up sempstress walks with hasty strides,
While streams run down her oiled umbrella's sides.
Here various kinds, by various fortunes led,
40   Commence acquaintance underneath a shed.
Triumphant Tories and desponding Whigs
Forget their feuds, and join to save their wigs.
Boxed in a chair the beau impatient sits,
While spouts run clattering o'er the roof by fits,
45   And ever and anon with frightful din
The leather sounds; he trembles from within.
So when Troy chairmen bore the wooden steed,
Pregnant with Greeks impatient to be freed
(Those bully Greeks, who, as the moderns do,
50   Instead of paying chairmen, run them through),
Laocoön struck the outside with his spear,
And each imprisoned hero quaked for fear.
    Now from all parts the swelling kennels flow,
And bear their trophies with them as they go:
55   Filth of all hues and odors seem to tell
What street they sailed from, by their sight and smell.
They, as each torrent drives, with rapid force,
From Smithfield or St. Pulchre's shape their course,
And in huge confluence joined at Snow Hill ridge,
60   Fall from the conduit prone to Holborn Bridge.
Sweepings from butchers' stalls, dung, guts, and blood,
Drowned puppies, stinking sprats, all drenched in mud,
Dead cats, and turnip-tops, come tumbling down the flood.

---

3 *depends:* threatens. 5 *sink:* sewer. 12 *spleen:* the blues. 13 *South:* south wind. 14 *welkin:* sky. 31 *contiguous:* close together. 35 *Templar:* student lawyer; *a-broach:* pouring. 43 *Boxed in a chair:* enclosed in a sedan chair, a kind of taxi carried on poles by two men. 46 *The leather:* the roof of the sedan chair, struck by water from the rain spouts. 47–52 *when Troy chairmen . . . quaked for fear:* Swift refers to an episode in Virgil's *Aeneid*, Book Two. The priest Laocoön, warning his fellow Trojans against the wooden horse in which enemy Greek soldiers were concealed, beat on the leather horse with his spear. 53 *kennels:* gutters. 62 *sprats:* herrings.

The Man-Moth*

             Here, above,
cracks in the buildings are filled with battered moonlight.
The whole shadow of Man is only as big as his hat.
It lies at his feet like a circle for a doll to stand on,
and he makes an inverted pin, the point magnetized to the moon.
He does not see the moon; he observes only her vast properties,
feeling the queer light on his hands, neither warm nor cold,
of a temperature impossible to record in thermometers.

             But when the Man-Moth
pays his rare, although occasional, visits to the surface,
the moon looks rather different to him. He emerges
from an opening under the edge of one of the sidewalks
and nervously begins to scale the faces of the buildings.
He thinks the moon is a small hole at the top of the sky,
proving the sky quite useless for protection.
He trembles, but must investigate as high as he can climb.

             Up the façades,
his shadow dragging like a photographer's cloth behind him,
he climbs fearfully, thinking that this time he will manage
to push his small head through that round clean opening
and be forced through, as from a tube, in black scrolls on the
       light.
(Man, standing below him, has no such illusions.)
But what the Man-Moth fears most he must do, although
he fails, of course, and falls back scared but quite unhurt.

             Then he returns
to the pale subways of cement he calls his home. He flits,
he flutters, and cannot get aboard the silent trains
fast enough to suit him. The doors close swiftly.
The Man-Moth always seats himself facing the wrong way
and the train starts at once at its full, terrible speed,
without a shift in gears or a gradation of any sort.
He cannot tell the rate at which he travels backwards.

*Newspaper misprint for "mammoth." [Author's note.]

44

                    Each night he must
be carried through artificial tunnels and dream recurrent
            dreams.
35 Just as the ties recur beneath his train, these underlie
his rushing brain. He does not dare look out the window,
for the third rail, the unbroken draught of poison,
runs there beside him. He regards it as a disease
he has inherited the susceptibility to. He has to keep
40 his hands in his pockets, as others must wear mufflers.

                    If you catch him,
hold up a flashlight to his eye. It's all dark pupil,
an entire night itself, whose haired horizon tightens
as he stares back, and closes up the eye. Then from the lids
45 one tear, his only possession, like the bee's sting, slips.
Slyly he palms it, and if you're not paying attention
he'll swallow it. However, it you watch, he'll hand it over,
cool as from underground springs and pure enough to drink.

The Dream

Someone approaches to say his life is ruined
and to fall down at your feet
and pound his head upon the sidewalk.
Blood spreads in a puddle.
And you, in a weak voice, plead
with those nearby for help;
your life takes on his desperation.
He keeps pounding his head.
It is you who are fated;
and you fall down beside him.
It is then you are awakened,
the body gone, the blood washed from the ground,
the stores lit up with their goods.

In a Mirror

A chance adjustment of my car mirror
Flashed in a broken sequence, first the dog,
The leash gripped in a gray glove,
Then the cane, stumbling over

5   Snow, a new mound. And then the man, the way
He turned his head. "I'm blind,"
It said, "I'm listening for the ground,
I hear you near me. Don't go away."

But I was gone, a block too far
10   To turn around, and it was late,
The hill steep and slick, and what
One other reason do I fumble over?

Thaw in the City

Now my legs begin to walk.
The filthy piles of snow are melting.
Pavements are wet.

What clear, tiny streams!
Suddenly I feel the blood flowing in the veins
in the backs of my hands.

And I hear a voice — a wonderful voice —
as if someone I loved had lifted a window
and called my name.

The streets wash over me like waves.
I sail in the boat of factories and sparrows
out of sight.

3. Earth Laughs in Flowers
Environments

Hamatreya

Bulkeley, Hunt, Willard, Hosmer, Meriam, Flint,
Possessed the land which rendered to their toil
Hay, corn, roots, hemp, flax, apples, wool and wood.
Each of these landlords walked amidst his farm,
Saying, ' 'Tis mine, my children's and my name's.
How sweet the west wind sounds in my own trees!
How graceful climb those shadows on my hill!
I fancy these pure waters and the flags
Know me, as does my dog: we sympathize;
And, I affirm, my actions smack of the soil.'

Where are these men? Asleep beneath their grounds:
And strangers, fond as they, their furrows plough.
Earth laughs in flowers, to see her boastful boys
Earth-proud, proud of the earth which is not theirs;
Who steer the plough, but cannot steer their feet
Clear of the grave.
They added ridge to valley, brook to pond,
And sighed for all that bounded their domain;
'This suits me for a pasture; that's my park;
We must have clay, lime, gravel, granite-ledge,
And misty lowland, where to go for peat.
The land is well, — lies fairly to the south.
'Tis good, when you have crossed the sea and back,
To find the sitfast acres where you left them.'
Ah! the hot owner sees not Death, who adds
Him to his land, a lump of mould the more.
Hear what the Earth says: —

Earth-Song

'Mine and yours;
Mine, not yours.
Earth endures;
Stars abide —
Shine down in the old sea;
Old are the shores;

53

But where are old men?
35   I who have seen much,
Such have I never seen.

'The lawyer's deed
Ran sure,
In tail,
40   To them, and to their heirs
Who shall succeed,
Without fail,
Forevermore.

'Here is the land,
45   Shaggy with wood,
With its old valley,
Mound and flood.
But the heritors? —
Fled like the flood's foam.
50   The lawyer, and the laws,
And the kingdom,
Clean swept herefrom.

'They called me theirs,
Who so controlled me;
55   Yet every one
Wished to stay, and is gone,
How am I theirs,
If they cannot hold me,
But I hold them?'

60   When I heard the Earth-song
I was no longer brave;
My avarice cooled
Like lust in the chill of the grave.

The title means "Earth-Mother." Emerson read the Hindu sacred scriptures
and apparently based this poem on a passage in the Vishnu Purana
that he copied into his journals in 1845: "These were the verses, Maitreya,
which Earth recited and by listening to which ambition fades away
like snow before the wind."

54

Working Against Time

By the newly bulldozed logging road, for a hundred yards,
I saw the sprawling five-foot hemlocks, their branches crammed
Into each other's light, upended or wrenched aslant
Or broken across waists the size of broomsticks
5   Or bent, crushed slewfoot on themselves in the duff like briars,
Their roots coming at random out of the dirt, and drying.

I had no burlap in the trunk, not even a spade,
And the shirt off my back wasn't enough to go around.
I'm no tree surgeon, it wasn't Arbor Day, but I climbed
10   Over the free-for-all, untangling winners and losers
And squeezing as many as I could into my car.
When I started, nothing was singing in the woods except me.

I hardly had room to steer — roots dangled over my shoulder
And scraped the side of my throat as if looking for water.
15   Branches against the fog on the windshield dabbled designs
Like kids or hung out the vent. The sun was falling down.
It's against the law to dig up trees. Working against
Time and across laws, I drove my ambulance

Forty miles in the dark to the house and began digging
20   Knee-deep graves for most of them, while the splayed headlights
Along the highway picked me out of the night:
A fool with a shovel searching for worms or treasure,
Both buried behind the sweat on his forehead. Two green
      survivors
Are tangled under the biting rain as I say this.

Why the soup tastes like the Daily News

The great dream stinks like a whale gone aground.
Somewhere in New York harbor
in the lee of the iron maiden
it died of pollution
5   and was cast up on Cape Cod by the Provincetown Light.
The vast blubber is rotting.
Scales of fat ripple over the waters
until the taste of it
like a sulphur yellow factory of chemical plenty
10   dyes every tongue.

All Watched Over by Machines of Loving Grace

I like to think (and
the sooner the better!)
of a cybernetic meadow
where mammals and computers
5   live together in mutually
programming harmony
like pure water
touching clear sky.

I like to think
10   (right now, please!)
of a cybernetic forest
filled with pines and electronics
where deer stroll peacefully
past computers
15   as if they were flowers
with spinning blossoms.

I like to think
(it has to be!)
of a cybernetic ecology
20   where we are free of our labors
and joined back to nature,
returned to our mammal
brothers and sisters,
and all watched over
25   by machines of loving grace.

Going Through

going through
Missouri once
a mocking bird
died against
my grill
5   and I
became a hearse
driver clear
to Kansas where
two children watched
10 me and no one
else had ever
seen a mocking
bird before

Smokey the Bear Sutra

Once in the Jurassic, about 150 million years ago,
the Great Sun Buddha in this corner of the Infinite
Void gave a great Discourse to all the assembled elements
and energies: to the standing beings, the walking beings,
the flying beings, and the sitting beings — even grasses,
to the number of thirteen billion, each one born from a
seed, were assembled there: a Discourse concerning
Enlightenment on the planet Earth.

"In some future time, there will be a continent called
America. It will have great centers of power called
such as Pyramid Lake, Walden Pond, Mt. Rainier, Big Sur,
Everglades, and so forth; and powerful nerves and channels
such as Columbia River, Mississippi River, and Grand
Canyon. The human race in that era will get into troubles all
over its head, and practically wreck everything in spite of its
own strong intelligent Buddha-nature."

"The twisting strata of the great mountains and the pulsings
of great volcanoes are my love burning deep in the earth. My
obstinate compassion is schist and basalt and granite, to be
mountains, to bring down the rain. In that future American
Era I shall enter a new form: to cure the world of loveless
knowledge that seeks with blind hunger, and mindless rage
eating food that will not fill it."

And he showed himself in his true form of

SMOKEY THE BEAR.

A handsome smokey-colored brown bear standing on his
hind legs, showing that he is aroused and watchful.

Bearing in his right paw the Shovel that digs to the
truth beneath appearances; cuts the roots of useless attach-
ments, and flings damp sand on the fires of greed and war;

His left paw in the Mudra of Comradely Display —
indicating that all creatures have the full right to live to
their limits and that deer, rabbits, chipmunks, snakes,
dandelions, and lizards all grow in the realm of the Dharma;

59

35   Wearing the blue work overalls symbolic of slaves and laborers, the countless men oppressed by a civilization that claims to save but only destroys;

Wearing the broad-brimmed hat of the West, symbolic of the forces that guard the Wilderness, which is the Natural
40   State of the Dharma and the True Path of man on earth; all true paths lead through mountains —

With a halo of smoke and flame behind, the forest fires of the kali-yuga, fires caused by the stupidity of those who think things can be gained and lost whereas in truth all is
45   contained vast and free in the Blue Sky and Green Earth of One Mind;

Round-bellied to show his kind nature and that the great earth has food enough for everyone who loves her and trusts her;

50   Trampling underfoot wasteful freeways and needless suburbs; smashing the worms of capitalism and totalitarianism;

Indicating the Task: his followers, becoming free of cars, houses, canned food, universities, and shoes, master the
55   Three Mysteries of their own Body, Speech, and Mind; and fearlessly chop down the rotten trees and prune out the sick limbs of this country America and then burn the leftover trash.

Wrathful but Calm, Austere but Comic, Smokey the Bear
60   will illuminate those who would help him; but for those who would hinder or slander him,

HE WILL PUT THEM OUT.

Thus his great Mantra:

Namah samanta vajranam chanda maharoshana
65   Sphataya hum traka ham mam

"I DEDICATE MYSELF TO THE UNIVERSAL
            DIAMOND
        BE THIS RAGING FURY DESTROYED"

And he will protect those who love woods and rivers, Gods
and animals, hobos and madmen, prisoners and sick people,
musicians, playful women, and hopeful children;

And if anyone is threatened by advertising, air pollution, or
the police, they should chant SMOKEY THE BEAR'S WAR
SPELL:

        DROWN THEIR BUTTS
        CRUSH THEIR BUTTS
        DROWN THEIR BUTTS
        CRUSH THEIR BUTTS

And SMOKEY THE BEAR will surely appear to put the
enemy out with his vajra-shovel.

Now those who recite this Sutra and then try to put it in
        practice will accumulate merit as countless as the sands
        of Arizona and Nevada,
Will help save the planet Earth from total oil slick,
Will enter the age of harmony of man and nature,
Will win the tender love and caresses of men, women, and
        beasts
Will always have ripe blackberries to eat and a sunny spot
        under a pine tree to sit at,

AND IN THE END WILL WIN HIGHEST PERFECT
        ENLIGHTENMENT.

                thus have we heard.

This work was first printed as a giveaway pamphlet with the note "may be
reproduced free forever."

61

Willy

Willy, enormous Saskatchewan grizzly — your blood partly
     polar,
tranquil your temper — with only your furred face visible
     in there
propped up over your puddle and pool-rim, scanning the
     crowd for
peanuts: we're all safe on humanity's side of your cage-bars.
One of your elbows sits on your concrete floor, with its huge paw
coyly supporting your chin, while your eyelids droop and your
     mouth hangs
cavernous, wide as a hillside, opening — heavens! — you're
     yawning.
Seeming so spiritless — so like a man — are you mocking
     us, Willy?

Nuts drop near you, and sometimes your free paw, big as a
     tree-stump,
mossy with air and with stick-sized claws on it, browned
     and decaying,
darts, and adroitly you sweep one into you, Willy — you're
     much too
civilized, playing obsequious tricks for these pestering people:
you have driven whole ox-herds before you through forests and
     ice fields.
Do you remember your long lone nights on the stardark tundra,
now that you're shut in from life and this wearying crowd
     and its clamors?
Bored, Willy? Who can awaken you? ("Up, Willy!" someone
     is calling.)
Peanuts may not be enough. Do you long for some tastier tribute?
That, Willy, needs a more godlike behavior and ("Up, Willy,
     up, up!")
dignity, Willy; more dignity's needed to ... Willy? What's
     moving?

Nothing is moving; yet all of you — face, paws, elbows —
    is rising.
Mountains of hair there are heaving up under you, streaming
    with waters,
up, up, up out of splashing cascades: dark shadowy body
up from the black earth's bubbling depths — and the women
    are shrieking.
How did they dare to confine you, those vermin alive on
    your shadow?
What is it makes you endure them, O swaying and perilous
    tower,
touching our day with a second of terror, our nights with a nasty
Freudian dream? How? — deftly you've caught it — that carton
    of — ice cream!

Song: Paper

Somebody told me I wouldn't know how to choose
Between presidential candidates if I didn't read the news,
And wouldn't even know who's out on bail for what crimes,
So I subscribed to the daily and the Sunday *Times*

5
     And all that paper piles up
     On the sofa, on the floor,
     In the wastebaskets and in front of the door,
     On the sills, and I can't see
     Out my window anymore.

I went through a magazine and clipped all the book-club
10
     come-ons
And they sent very friendly bills and then they threatened to
     send a summons,
And they kept sending me monthly selections, and alternates,
     and when
I wrote them to stop they didn't but they billed me again

     And all that paper. . . .

15
The other day I hunted in every corner of every drawer
Our marriage certificate, though I can't remember just what for,
And I found old notebooks and loose sheets and scraps in
     illegible condition
And both our lives scribbled out and wadded in every
     conceivable position

     And all that paper. . . .

20
And while I was digging around, at the back of a bottom shelf
I came across a dog-eared spineless mildewed *Song of Myself,*
So I gave it to a friend and in return for what I'd given
He sent me a complete *Congressional Record* back to 1867

     And all that paper. . . .

Rivers are clogging with *Time, Life, Evergreen,* and other soggy
wisdom;
Some high official in Washington just misfiled the key to the
filing system;
I can never find my driver's license among all the credit cards
and such;
You can die for lack of paper or you can die from too much.

And all that paper piles up
On the sofa, on the floor,
In the wastebaskets and in front of the door,
On the sills, and I can't see
Out my window anymore.

25

30

The Town Dump

"The art of our necessities is strange,
That can make vile things precious."

A mile out in the marshes, under a sky
Which seems to be always going away
In a hurry, on that Venetian land threaded
With hidden canals, you will find the city
Which seconds ours (so cemeteries, too,
Reflect a town from hillsides out of town),
Where Being most Becomingly ends up
Becoming some more. From cardboard tenements,
Windowed with cellophane, or simply tenting
In paper bags, the angry mackerel eyes
Glare at you out of stove-in, sunken heads
Far from the sea; the lobster, also, lifts
An empty claw in his most minatory
Of gestures; oyster, crab, and mussel shells
Lie here in heaps, savage as money hurled
Away at the gate of hell. If you want results,
These are results.
                        Objects of value or virtue,
However, are also to be picked up here,
Though rarely, lying with bones and rotten meat,
Eggshells and mouldy bread, banana peels
No one will skid on, apple cores that caused
Neither the fall of man nor a theory
Of gravitation. People do throw out
The family pearls by accident, sometimes,
Not often; I've known dealers in antiques
To prowl this place by night, with flashlights, on
The off-chance of somebody's having left
Derelict chairs which will turn out to be
By Hepplewhite, a perfect set of six
Going to show, I guess, that in any sty
Someone's heaven may open and shower down
Riches responsive to the right dream; though
It is a small chance, certainly, that sends

The ghostly dealer, heavy with fly-netting
35 Over his head, across these hills in darkness,
Stumbling in cut-glass goblets, lacquered cups,
And other products of his dreamy midden
Penciled with light and guarded by the flies.

For there are flies, of course. A dynamo
40 Composed, by thousands, of our ancient black
Retainers, hums here day and night, steady
As someone telling beads, the hum becoming
A high whine at any disturbance; then,
Settled again, they shine under the sun
45 Like oil-drops, or are invisible as night,
By night.
          All this continually smoulders,
Crackles, and smokes with mostly invisible fires
Which, working deep, rarely flash out and flare,
And never finish. Nothing finishes;
50 The flies, feeling the heat, keep on the move.

Among the flies, the purifying fires,
The hunters by night, acquainted with the art
Of our necessities, and the new deposits
That each day wastes with treasure, you may say
55 There should be ratios. You may sum up
The results, if you want results. But I will add
That wild birds, drawn to the carrion and flies,
Assemble in some numbers here, their wings
Shining with light, their flight enviably free,
60 Their music marvelous, though sad, and strange.

Death-Lace

With deathlace tickling my throat
I'm bulb-eyed at midnight
To remember whole afternoons of causes —
Charley Pape and the '35 Dodge
5   Opening it up, and all those giggling girls.
Before I was old enough. And idling too.
I turned around once when his friends
Were in the backseat. That's the past
Those girls sitting on tavern stools when
10   Charley stops in to pick them up, revs the Dodge
And roars down his favorite road.
I'm old enough now and have saved nothing
From that year but its contribution
To deathlace. Roads I can't remember riding
15   Down. And the quaint odor of flyspray
Around my grandfather's clock
With its gilt painting on the face, an ad.
The Expressways, with their share
For each taxpayer, share of the modern death.
20   These are the death-flies hovering
Around my curls, sneaking a bite
At my tense neck of Apollo.
They are not ordinary flies
On the pink stucco; they are put out
25   By Standard Oil along with green stamps
And dinosaur balloons; they are a part
Of the deathlace. Peering down
Into my fish gullet even now you might fail
To see it, like a fine crochet or Queen Anne's
30   On a salmon slope in Oklahoma. Highway 66
I've gulped it there. Deathlace
From Dodge, Ford, Pontiac, Studebaker.
It floated in from downtown one night
So coughing thick I thought it was L.A.'s
35   Bookstore stripjoint slums I was 2 blocks from
Instead of an Upstate valley town with a few
Taverns bobbing their blinkers, neons

Wobbling down the long red necklace
Of Elmina Road. Winter, and everyone leaves
40 A little deathlace running while buying stamps
Or wandering the dimestore. It's a gift
To children in strollers and to poets
And to fish and the upper atmosphere
And the doctors and shoeclerks have added
45 Deathlace looking for deathlace or swollen
Metatarsals. But mostly deathlace has been added
Just for fun. Or the profit on the Eastman film.
Charley with the motor running and that girl goosed.

The Blue Whale

Three hugest dinosaurs do not outweigh
That one hundred foot long whale who will strain
The sea for krill, four tons a day. Svend Foyn,
A man, found how to blow its twenty pound brain
To rice and still its thousand pound heart
For its forty thousand pounds of oil. Soon
The blue whale fewer than the whooping crane
Will be, who is a useless bird. Of old,
Churchmen said the devil was like a whale.
Soon we can sail dry seas empty of all
Monstrosities, and man alone can strain
The little krill, all food, thought for his brain.
There's life some say in smallest grains of rice.
Man must eat; killing is not good, not evil.
After waters are plundered well as land,
I will think
Of Svend Foyn who destroyed the devil,
A one hundred and fifty ton, toothless blue whale.

3 *Svend Foyn:* Norwegian whaler whose invention of the harpoon gun, about the year 1860, revolutionized the whaling industry.

The Pond

With nets and kitchen sieves they raid the pond,
Chasing the minnows into bursts of mud,
Scooping and chopping, raking up frond after frond
Of swollen weed after a week of flood.

5   Thirty or forty minnows bob and flash
In every jam-jar hoarded on the edge,
While the shrill children with each ill-aimed splash
Haul out another dozen as they dredge.

Choked to its banks, the pond spills out its store
10   Of frantic life. Nothing can drain it dry
Of what it breeds: it breeds so effortlessly
Theft seems to leave it richer than before.

The nostrils snuff its rank bouquet — how warm,
How lavish, foul and indiscriminate, fat
15   With insolent appetite and thirst, so that
The stomach almost heaves to see it swarm.

But trapped in glass the minnows flail and fall,
Sink, with upended bellies showing white.
After an hour I look and see that all
20   But four or five have died. The greenish light

Ripples to stillness, while the children bend
To spoon the corpses out, matter-of-fact,
Absorbed: as if creation's prodigal act
Shrank to this empty jam-jar in the end.

The World Below the Brine

The world below the brine,
Forests at the bottom of the sea, the branches and leaves,
Sea-lettuce, vast lichens, strange flowers and seeds, the thick
    tangle, openings, and pink turf,
Different colors, pale gray and green, purple, white, and gold,
    the play of light through the water,

Dumb swimmers there among the rocks, coral, gluten, grass,
    rushes, and the aliment of the swimmers,
Sluggish existences grazing there suspended, or slowly crawling
    close to the bottom,
The sperm-whale at the surface blowing air and spray, or
    disporting with his flukes,
The leaden-eyed shark, the walrus, the turtle, the hairy sea-
    leopard, and the sting-ray,
Passions there, wars, pursuits, tribes, sight in those ocean-depths,
    breathing that thick-breathing air, as so many do,
The change thence to the sight here, and to the subtle air
    breathed by beings like us who walk this sphere,
The change onward from ours to that of beings who walk other
    spheres.

Looking into a Tide Pool

It is a tide pool, shallow, water coming in, clear, tiny white shell-people on the bottom, asking nothing, not even directions! On the surface the noduled seaweed, lying like hands, slowly drawing back and returning, hands laid on fevered bodies, moving back and forth, as the healer sings wildly, shouting to Jesus and his dead mother.

Pike

Pike, three inches long, perfect
Pike in all parts, green tigering the gold.
Killers from the egg: the malevolent aged grin.
They dance on the surface among the flies.

5   Or move, stunned by their own grandeur,
Over a bed of emerald, silhouette
Of submarine delicacy and horror.
A hundred feet long in their world.

In ponds, under the heat-struck lily pads —
10   Gloom of their stillness:
Logged on last year's black leaves, watching upwards.
Or hung in an amber cavern of weeds

The jaws' hooked clamp and fangs
Not to be changed at this date;
15   A life subdued to its instrument;
The gills kneading quietly, and the pectorals.

Three we kept behind glass,
Jungled in weed: three inches, four,
And four and a half: fed fry to them —
20   Suddenly there were two. Finally one

With a sag belly and the grin it was born with.
And indeed they spare nobody.
Two, six pounds each, over two feet long,
High and dry and dead in the willow-herb —

25   One jammed past its gills down the other's gullet:
The outside eye stared: as a vice locks —
The same iron in this eye
Though its film shrank in death.

A pond I fished, fifty yards across,
30   Whose lilies and muscular tench
Had outlasted every visible stone
Of the monastery that planted them —

Stilled legendary depth:
It was as deep as England. It held
Pike too immense to stir, so immense and old
That past nightfall I dared not cast

But silently cast and fished
With the hair frozen on my head
For what might move, for what eye might move.
The still splashes on the dark pond,

Owls hushing the floating woods
Frail on my ear against the dream
Darkness beneath night's darkness had freed,
That rose slowly towards me, watching.

Morels

A wet gray day — rain falling slowly, mist over the valley,
    mountains dark circumflex smudges in the distance —

Apple blossoms just gone by, the branches feathery still
    as if fluttering with half-visible antennae —

A day in May like so many in these green mountains, and
    I went out just as I had last year

At the same time, and found them there under the big maples —
    by the bend in the road — right where they had stood

Last year and the year before that, risen from the dark duff
    of the woods, emerging at odd angles

From spores hidden by curled and matted leaves, a fringe of
    rain on the grass around them,

Beads of rain on the mounded leaves and mosses round them,

Not in a ring themselves but ringed by jack-in-the-pulpits
    with deep eggplant-colored stripes;

Not ringed but rare, not gilled but polyp-like, having
    sprung up overnight —

These mushrooms of the gods, resembling human organs
    uprooted, rooted only on the air,

Looking like lungs wrenched from the human body, lungs
    reversed, not breathing internally

But being the externalization of breath itself, these
    spicy, twisted cones,

These perforated brown-white asparagus tips — these morels,
    smelling of wet graham crackers mixed with maple leaves;

And, reaching down by the pale green fern shoots, I nipped
    their pulpy stems at the base

And dropped them into a paper bag — a damp brown bag (their
    color) — and carried

76

Them (weighing absolutely nothing) down the hill and into
    the house; you held them

Under cold bubbling water and sliced them with a surgeon's
    stroke clean through,

And sautéed them over a low flame, butter-brown; and we ate
    them then and there —

Tasting of the sweet damp woods and of the rain one inch
    above the meadow:

20   It was like feasting upon air.

Directive

Back out of all this now too much for us,
Back in a time made simple by the loss
Of detail, burned, dissolved, and broken off
Like graveyard marble sculpture in the weather,
There is a house that is no more a house
Upon a farm that is no more a farm
And in a town that is no more a town.
The road there, if you'll let a guide direct you
Who only has at heart your getting lost,
May seem as if it should have been a quarry —
Great monolithic knees the former town
Long since gave up pretense of keeping covered.
And there's a story in a book about it:
Besides the wear of iron wagon wheels
The ledges show lines ruled southeast northwest,
The chisel work of an enormous Glacier
That braced his feet against the Arctic Pole.
You must not mind a certain coolness from him
Still said to haunt this side of Panther Mountain.
Nor need you mind the serial ordeal
Of being watched from forty cellar holes
As if by eye pairs out of forty firkins.
As for the woods' excitement over you
That sends light rustle rushes to their leaves,
Charge that to upstart inexperience.
Where were they all not twenty years ago?
They think too much of having shaded out
A few old pecker-fretted apple trees.
Make yourself up a cheering song of how
Someone's road home from work this once was,
Who may be just ahead of you on foot
Or creaking with a buggy load of grain.
The height of the adventure is the height
Of country where two village cultures faded
Into each other. Both of them are lost.
And if you're lost enough to find yourself

By now, pull in your ladder road behind you
And put a sign up CLOSED to all but me.
Then make yourself at home. The only field
Now left's no bigger than a harness gall.
First there's the children's house of make believe,
Some shattered dishes underneath a pine,
The playthings in the playhouse of the children.
Weep for what little things could make them glad.
Then for the house that is no more a house,
But only a belilaced cellar hole,
Now slowly closing like a dent in dough.
This was no playhouse but a house in earnest.
Your destination and your destiny's
A brook that was the water of the house,
Cold as a spring as yet so near its source,
Too lofty and original to rage.
(We know the valley streams that when aroused
Will leave their tatters hung on barb and thorn.)
I have kept hidden in the instep arch
Of an old cedar at the waterside
A broken drinking goblet like the Grail
Under a spell so the wrong ones can't find it,
So can't get saved, as Saint Mark says they mustn't.
(I stole the goblet from the children's playhouse.)
Here are your waters and your watering place.
Drink and be whole again beyond confusion.

The Sun Wields Mercy

and the sun wields mercy
but like a torch carried too high,
and the jets whip across its sight
and rockets leap like toads,
5   and the boys get out the maps
and pin-cushion the moon,
old green cheese,
no life there but too much on earth:
our unwashed India boys
10 crossing their legs, playing pipes,
starving with sucked-in bellies,
watching the snakes volute
like beautiful women in the hungry air;
the rockets leap,
15 the rockets leap like hares,
clearing clump and dog
and out-dated bullets;
the Chinese still carve
in jade, quietly stuffing rice
20 into their hunger, a hunger
a thousand years old,
their muddy rivers moving with fire
and song, barges, houseboats
pushed by the drifting poles
25 of waiting without wanting;
in Turkey they face the East
on their carpets
praying to a purple god
who smokes and laughs
30 and sticks his fingers in their eyes
blinding them, as gods will do;

but the rockets are ready: peace is no longer,
for some reason, precious;
madness drifts like lily pads
35 on a pond, circling senselessly;
the painters paint dipping

80

their reds and greens and yellows,
poets rhyme their loneliness,
musicians starve as always
40 and the novelists miss the mark,
but not the pelican, the gull;
pelicans dip and dive, rise,
shaking shocked half-dead
radioactive fish from their beaks;
45 indeed, indeed, the waters wash
the rocks with slime; and Wall St,
the market staggers like a lost drunk
looking for his key; ah,
this will be a good one, by God:
50 it will take us back to the
snake, the limpet, or if we're lucky,
the catalysis to the
sabre-tooth, the winged monkey
scrabbling in the pit over bits
55 of helmet, instrument and glass;
a lightning crashes across
the window and in a million rooms
lovers lie entwined and lost
and sick as peace;
60 the sky breaks red and orange for the
painters — and for the lovers,
flowers open as they have always
opened but covered with the thin dust
of rocket fuel and mushrooms,
65 poison mushrooms; it's a bad time,
a dog-sick time — curtain,
act III, standing room only,
SOLD OUT, SOLD OUT, SOLD OUT again,
by god, by somebody and something,
70 by rockets and generals and
leaders, by poets, doctors, comedians,
by manufacturers of soup
and biscuits, Janus-faced hucksters

81

of their own indexterity;
75 I can see now the coal-slick
contaminated fields, a snail or 2,
bile, obsidian, a fish or 3
in the shallows, an obloquy of our
source and our sight . . .
80 has this happened before? history
could be a circle that catches itself,
a dream, a nightmare,
a general's dream, a president's dream,
a dictator's dream . . .
85 can't we awaken?
or are the forces of life greater than we?
can't we awaken? must we forever,
dear friends, die in our sleep?

4. Suburb and Secret Valley
Life Styles

The Lingam and the Yoni

The Lingam and the Yoni
Are walking hand in glove,
O are you listening, honey?
I hear my honey-love.

5 The He and She our movers
What is it they discuss?
Is it the talk of Lovers?
And do they speak of us?

I hear their high palaver —
10 O tell me what they say!
The talk goes on for ever
So deep in love are they.

So deep in thought, debating
The suburb and the street;
15 Time-payment calculating
Upon the bedroom suite.

But ours is long division
By love's arithmetic,
Until they make provision
20 To buy a box of brick,

A box that makes her prisoner,
That he must slave to win
To do the Lingam honor,
To keep the Yoni in.

25 The mortgage on tomorrow?
The haemorrhage of rent?
Against the heart they borrow
At five or six per cent.

The heart has bought fulfillment
30 Which yet their mouths defer
Until the last installment
Upon the furniture.

No Lingam for her money
Can make up youth's arrears:
His layby on the Yoni
Will not be paid in years.

And they, who keep this tally,
They count what they destroy;
While, in its secret valley,
Withers the herb of joy.

35

40

I went into the Maverick Bar

I went into the Maverick Bar
In Farmington, New Mexico.
And drank double shots of bourbon,
               backed with beer.
My long hair was tucked up under a cap
I'd left the earring in the car.

Two cowboys did horseplay
               by the pool tables,
A waitress asked us
               where are you from?
A country-and-western band began to play
"We don't smoke Marijuana in Muskokie"
And with the next song,
               a couple began to dance.

They held each other like in High School dances
               in the fifties;
I recalled when I worked in the woods
               and the bars of Madras, Oregon.
That short-haired joy and roughness —
               America — your stupidity.
I could almost love you again.

We left — onto the freeway shoulders —
               under the tough old stars —
In the shadow of bluffs
               I came back to myself,
To the real work, to
               "What is to be done."

Black Jack Davey

Black Jack Davey come ridin' through the woods,
Singin' so loud and merry
That the green hills all around him ring,
And he charmed the heart of a lady.

5 "How old are you, my pretty little miss,
How old are you, my lady?"
She answered him with a "Tee, hee, hee,
I'll be sixteen next summer."

"Come, go with me, my pretty little miss,
10 Come, go with me, my lady;
I'll take you across the deep blue sea
Where you never shall want for money.

"Won't you pull off those high heeled shoes
All made of Spanish leather;
15 Won't you put on some low heeled shoes?
And we'll ride off together."

She soon pulled off those high heeled shoes
All made of Spanish leather;
She put on those low heeled shoes
20 And they rode off together.

'Twas late at night when the land-lord come
Inquirin' for his lady.
He was posted by a fair young maid:
"She's gone with Black Jack Davey."

25 "Go saddle me my noble steed,
Go bridle me my derby;
I'll ride to the east, I'll ride to the west,
Or overtake my lady."

He rode till he came to the deep below;
30 The stream was deep and muddy.
Tears came tricklin' down his cheeks,
For there he spied his lady.

"How can you leave your house and land,
How can you leave your baby,
35 How can you leave your husband dear
To go with Black Jack Davey?"

"Very well can I leave my house and land,
Very well can I leave my baby,
Much better can I leave my husband dear
40 To go with Black Jack Davey.

"I won't come back to you, my love,
Nor I won't come back, my husband;
I wouldn't give a kiss from Davey's lips
For all your land and money.

45 "Last night I lay on a feather bed
Beside my husband and baby;
Tonight I lay on the cold damp ground
Beside the Black Jack Davey."

She soon run through her gay clothing,
50 Her velvet shoes and stockings;
Her gold ring off her finger was gone,
And the gold plate off her bosom.

"Oh, once I had a house and land,
A feather bed and money,
55 But now I've come to an old straw pad,
With nothing but Black Jack Davey."

This is a southern American folk version of the traditional Scottish
ballad "The Gypsy Laddie."

91

Hose and Iron

It was always
father with the hose
and mother with the iron

then later it was
father with the iron
mother with the hose

but it was always
the hose and the iron

First, the hose:

Father said,
"when I was in
chemistry
this little guy came in
and all the wiseapples
were wisecracking
so he took out his hose
and banged on the desk
everybody shut up."

"The only way to treat kids."

Mother said,
"do you want your socks ironed
your pants ironed
your shirts
if you want those shirts ironed today
put them out for me
don't leave them balled up
on the stairway."

A long heavy hose
as big around as an arm
whack
they shut up

square shirts
pink yellow striped shirts
nice shirts

35   Hose me father
make me mind
hose me

iron me mother
I need to be ironed out

40   Father mother
I am dying of wisecracks

The Work-out

I am dressed in my old grey running suit.
I have a towel for sweat and a jockstrap
because my fear is great. I will myself

out onto the track to join you,
hurdling and sprinting the countryside,
because you can not wait for me.

I envy your directness and speed —
I bet you were the fastest runner
in the sixth grade — and your control!

You move right out along the blades
of your slicing vision.
I must accept the limits

of a slower pace. I'm in it
for distance . . . no special
regimens or diet, thank you,

just a normal growth. No breakthroughs.
You with your pounding nervous strength,
committed to great leaps and deep breaths,

bolt out, driven by laughing
or crying. Your exertion makes me gasp.
But I long for your pace:

no doubts, no hesitation, just
the plunge forward, the awful
crashing and surging of the new.

Song

She was lyin face down in her face
On her eyelids stood the humanopolis race
The Chain-Janes were sleepin around
But they remembered to cheer when the police drowned

So thousands sitting on the slope listen to me
I'm goin back to the old chapel in the dew
Gonna be free from that there 28th Amendment
Says I got to smile when I kill you

I'm here tomorrow and gone today
I don't care what the pioneers say
They'll never get me to kill for my pay
Cause I'll be here tomorrow but I'm gone
I'll be here tomorrow but I'm gone
I'll be here tomorrow but I'm gone
Today

It was a long hot summers night
You can lock me up and throw the tears away
I've had nothing but the best since the pearly night
She came and took me away

To her little cabin in the woods we roamed
Her many children stood in the doorway wavin us in
In my Father's house there is many a home
And in every one of them there's no way out

I'm here tomorrow and gone today
I don't care what the pioneers say
They say they want me to be a saint
They say I'll be here tomorrow but I'm gone
Yes I'm here tomorrow but I'm gone
So gone
I'm here tomorrow and gone
Today

So comeon and spank me with a needle of closeups
I'm not buyin I'm only windowshoppin
Rolla coupla mummies from the stash in your stockings
I looked in the mirror before I was born but I didn't see nothin

95

Cocaine Lil

Did you ever hear about Cocaine Lil?
She lived in Cocaine town on Cocaine Hill,
She had a cocaine dog and a cocaine cat,
They fought all night with a cocaine rat.

5   She had cocaine hair on her cocaine head.
She had a cocaine dress that was poppy red;
She wore a snowbird hat and sleigh-riding clothes.
On her coat she wore a crimson, cocaine rose.

Big gold chariots on the Milky Way,
10   Snakes and elephants silver and gray.
Oh the cocaine blues they make me sad,
Oh the cocaine blues make me feel bad.

Lil went to a snow party one cold night,
And the way she sniffed was sure a fright.
15   There was Hophead Mag with Dopey Slim,
Kankakee Liz and Yen Shee Jim.

There was Morphine Sue and the Poppy Face Kid,
Climbed up snow ladders and down they slid;
There was the Stepladder Kid, a good six feet,
20   And the Sleigh-riding Sisters who were hard to beat.

Along in the morning about half past three
They were all lit up like a Christmas tree;
Lil got home and started for bed,
Took another sniff and it knocked her dead.

25   They laid her out in her cocaine clothes:
She wore a snowbird hat with a crimson rose;
On her headstone you'll find this refrain:
"She died as she lived, sniffing cocaine."

Motorcycle Irene

There she sits a'-smokin'
Reefer in her mouth.
Her hair hanging northward
As she travels south.
5   Dirty, on her Harley,
(But her nails are clean.)
Super-powered, de-flowered,
Over-eighteen Irene.

I've seen her in the bare
10 Where her tatoos and her chains
Wrap around her body,
Where written are the names
Of prisons she's been in,
And lovers she has seen,
15 Curve-winding, bumping, grinding,
Motorcycle Irene.

Ground round like hamburger
Laying in a splat
'Tis Irene, her sheen I seen
20 In pieces crumpled flat.
Her feet were in the bushes,
Her toes were in her hat,
Stark-ravin', un-shaven
Motorcycle Irene.

25 The Hunchback, the Cripple,
The Horseman, and the Fool,
Prayer books and candles, and
Carpets, cloaks, and jewels,
Knowing all the answers
30 Breaking all the rules,
With stark naked, unsacred,
Motorcycle Irene.

Hemmed-in Males

The saloon is gone up the creek
with the black sand round its
mouth, it went floating like

a backhouse on the Mississippi in
flood time but it went up
the creek into Limbo from whence

only empty bottles ever return
and that's where George is
He's gone upstream to ask 'em

to let him in at the hole
in the wall where the W.C.T.U.
sits knitting elastic stockings

for varicose veins. Poor George
he's got a job now as janitor
in Lincoln School but the saloon

is gone forever with pictures
of Sullivan and Kilrain on
the walls and Pop Anson holding

a bat. Poor George, they've cut
out his pituitary gland and his
vas deferens is in the spittoon —

You can laugh at him without his
organs but that's the way with
a river when it wants to

drown you, it sucks you in and
you feel the old saloon sinking
under you and you say good-by

just as George did, good-by poetry
the black sand's got me, the old
30   days are over, there's no place

any more for me to go now
except home —

11 *W.C.T.U.:* Woman's Christian Temperance Union.   17 *Sullivan
and Kilrain:* John L. Sullivan, heavyweight boxing champion from 1882 to
1892, and (Williams probably means) Johnny Kilbane, featherweight
champion from 1912 to 1923.   18 *Pop Anson:* Cap Anson (1852–1922), Hall
of Fame first baseman.   21 *vas deferens:* duct that carries sperm out
of the testicles.

The Misery of Mechanics

The misery of mechanics, back
after Labor Day, with nothing

to punch but the Time Clock:
somebody's wife has a squeak

5   in her new right-rear door;
an old professor phones in

for his first State Inspection.
Dry-tongued with pushbutton

coffee, shapeless in cover-
10   alls, each of a thousand

mechanics, all over town,
pushes darkly in under

the oil pan, drained as he
elbows his creeper to work.

*

15   Repairing himself to sleep,
wrenching his nails with soapstone,

he washes his hands of Chevys,
zips carefully, and punches

out: Dodges are still
20   expensive, Fords too cheap

to be worth repair. Driving
the daily bridge from Men's Room

to wife, he figures the whole
damn job, the complete over-

25   haul, at the usual flat rate:
         bridges, marriages, used

         car lots — his mechanic's
         eye sees that the parts are all there;

         it is, in fact, already jacked up.
30   But nothing that he can fix.

Crew-cuts

Men with crew-cuts
are impossible, like
ice shows. In airport bars, all winter,
holding stand-by tickets,
they wait for a plane into the next territory
and confess
to puzzlement
over the Oriental mind.

Later, they want to drop eggs on the Russians.
Later, they want
to keep violence out of the streets
by installing a machine-gun-nest on every corner.
When they talk about women, they are discussing
a subjugated race
rumored to have cached away
huge quantities of ammunition.
They lounge on the porch of the Planter's Club,
in darkest Africa,
pith helmets over their crew-cuts, drinking pink gins,
and laughing at jokes about the stupid natives,

while the tom-toms start to beat
in a million kitchens,
and the sky lightens
with a storm of Russians with hair
down to their shoulders,
as inscrutable as the Chinese,
and as merciless
as women.

The Function Room

We worked in the kitchen
of the function room,
me and black Jackson
and the cook, he's Vince.
5   We waxed the linoleum
and set out the frills
for the chromium people
who came to those
Friday night functions.

10   Six hundred kumquats
rolled in pastrami,
Green frou-frou toothpicks or red?
(Isn't that some of
black Jackson's shrimp salad
15   stuck there on that cummerbund?)
Each function night you could
smell the hair tonic
from out in the parking lot.

After the party we
20   gathered up lipsticks
left in the ladies' room.
We swept up the chicory,
we played with the olives.
I took some shrimp salad
25   home for my cat,
but he wouldn't eat it,
so I quit.

The Blue-eyed Precinct Worker

Liberal, blue-eyed, shivering, trying not
to look like a bill
collector or detective,
I move through the slums in a drizzle —
the slums of Pasadena, where — nutmeg, bronze,
and purple — the Negroes live.

They look out and laugh — Mrs. Bessie Simpson,
Miss Delilah Jones,
the eleven Tollivers.
They are extras in a bad movie
starring no one they have ever seen before,
no one that they care to know.

I am like a man rich in the currency
of a lost kingdom,
for this both is and is not
what I sought. Somewhere, a screen door bangs
and bangs, but in the half-light I can't see where,
or give the sound direction.

A black and white sausage of a mongrel bitch
follows me, sniffing;
her obscene stump of a tail
motionless. We go, the two of us,
to the muddy edge of the dark arroyo.
The street light blooms overhead;

our shadows burst forth monstrous and alien.
There, on the far rim,
are the houses of the rich.
It is the dinner hour, and they eat
prime rib of unicorn, or breast of phoenix.
It is another precinct.

Oddly enough, I am consoled by the thought
of the delicate
small animals that move down
through the arroyo: white coyote,
35   masked coon, and the plumed skunk. Come, Citizen Dog,
we have chosen the short straw.

In 1876
The Cooper & Bailey Great London Circus
Sailing from *Tasmania* to *Australia*
Suffered *Grievous* Injuries
5   During A Storm of *Singular* Magnitude

The *Rhinoceros* and The *Lion*
And The *Alligator* and The *Silver Fox*
And The *Tattooed Mule* and The *Imitation*
Penguin and The *Whitewashed Elephant*
10   Were Among Those *Drowned*
In The *Bubbling* Pacific

Cunning James Bailey
Had The Waterlogged *Giraffe*
Stuffed by A Gentleman in Sydney
15   Its *Head* Equipped with A *Device*
That Made It *Nod* Slowly and Regularly
Wily Bailey
Showed The Beast in A *Darkened Cage*
And It *Appeared* to Be *Alive* Which Made
20   The *Australian People*
Very Very Happy
And So They *Remain* to This Day
A *Grand* Triumph for The *Grand* Bailey
Mourner of Rhino *Fisher* of Lion
25   *Resurrector of Giraffe*
The *Bold* and *Businesslike* Bailey
Who *Gave* The People What They *Wanted*

This Has Been A Demanding Quarter
For Your Company   Sales Decreased 14
30   *Percent over The Corresponding Period*
A Year Ago   Nevertheless
We Are Pleased To Tell You That
Net Earnings (There Was A Fire
In Ohio In Which Several Clowns
35   Burned Up) *More Than Held Their Own*
Hold Your Own   Hold Her Own
Hold His Own   Nod Your Head

Much Madness is divinest Sense

Much Madness is divinest Sense –
To a discerning Eye –
Much Sense – the starkest Madness –
'Tis the Majority
In this, as All, prevail –
Assent – and you are sane –
Demur – you're straightway dangerous –
And handled with a Chain –

In the Suburbs

There's no way out.
You were born to waste your life.
You were born to this middleclass life

As others before you
Were born to walk in procession
To the temple, singing.

The Poor Old Prurient Interest Blues

Napoleon is standing with his pants upon the floor
There are naked, the painted people in the poster on my door
John Lennon and his girl friend couldn't show me any more
Won't someone please arouse my prurient int'rest?

There's flesh throughout my magazines, it ripples thick and
5 smooth
Ah, the door fell off the bathroom now I see what all you do
As I grab my flannel fig leaf just to keep from being rude
Have mercy on my poor old prurient int'rest.

Chorus:

Won't you let me look myself instead of waving it at me
10 Don't leave it hanging out and sagging over ev'ry thing I see
Don't take it off till I'm ready, let me have my little dreams
Have mercy on my poor old prurient int'rests.

There's somethin back behind me so I quickly turn around
The muffled sound of underwear as it comes tumblin down
15 Someone else is goin natural do I have to turn around
Have mercy on my poor old prurient interest.

110

Six-forty-two farm commune
struggle Poem

Fresh day cracks, goat's milkspurt
jinging the fishscale pail. She
chomps dead pussywillows, me, haven't even
had my brownrice yet, lastnight's tea.

5   Muzzey is gone. Out. Persuaded to
move on — too many footwashes
in the maple-farmer's brook, ripping off
too-little stores.
               The Town
stares through their glasses when you go in
10   shopping, you, worm on their overalls!

Got to make
            Burlington today, find
well-settler. Hoisting water mucked
like my mind. Click the barndoor shut,
gray board
15   splitting like open palms, Marilou
in her busted onebutton pyjamas stirring
in the kitchen stirring rice stew, kiss
her neck.
          Where's chow?
              Me.
Only way, says Max: sling
20   self on the trash like corncobs, open, be.

Marilou,
your breath smells
stale raisins and good cookies, why does my
sleepingbag crave the spikeweed path
25   to soak me deep in
self-leftovers? Regardless of who
the Chart says sleeps with you
I'm sleeping alone tonight.

Poverty

When I looked at my poverty:
My boots and the belly of my wife,
The mouse lying in the trap,
And the face of my son while he sleeps,
I knew nothing can hurt me any longer.
I can set out into the night
Without hope,
Without direction.

Nothing can hurt me any longer.
I know I live.

It is a gift
Which I am no longer afraid
To open.

5. One-Half of Humanity
Identity of a Woman

Two Sections from "Pro Femina"

I take as my theme, "The Independent Woman"

I take as my theme, "The Independent Woman,"
Independent but maimed: observe the exigent neckties
Choking violet writers; the sad slacks of stipple-faced
     matrons;
Indigo intellectuals, crop-haired and callous-toed,
Cute spectacles, chewed cuticles, aced out by full-time
5   beauties
In the race for a male. Retreating to drabness, bad manners
And sleeping with manuscripts. Forgive our transgressions
Of old gallantries as we hitch in chairs, light our own
     cigarettes,
Not expecting your care, having forfeited it by trying to get
     even.

10 But we need dependency, cosseting and well-treatment.
So do men sometimes. Why don't they admit it?
We will be cows for a while, because babies howl for us,
Be kittens or bitches, who want to eat grass now and then
For the sake of our health. But the role of pastoral heroine
15 Is not permanent, Jack. We want to get back to the meeting.

Knitting booties and brows, tartars or termagants, ancient
Fertility symbols, chained to our cycle, released
Only in part by devices of hygiene and personal daintiness,
Strapped into our girdles, held down, yet uplifted by man's
20 Ingenious constructions, holding coiffures in a breeze,
Hobbled and swathed in whimsey, tripping on feminine
Shoes with fool heels, losing our lipsticks, you, me,
In ephemeral stockings, clutching our handbags and
     packages.

Our masks, always in peril of smearing or cracking,
25 In need of continuous check in the mirror or silverware,
Keep us in thrall to ourselves, concerned with our surfaces.
Look at man's uniform drabness, his impersonal envelope!
Over chicken wrists or meek shoulders, a formal, hard-fibered
     assurance.

117

The drape of the male is designed to achieve self-
        forgetfulness.

So, sister, forget yourself a few times and see where it gets
        you:
Up the creek, alone with your talent, sans everything else.
You can wait for the menopause, and catch up on your
        reading.
So primp, preen, prink, pluck and prize your flesh,
All posturings! All ravishment! All sensibility!
Meanwhile, have you used your mind today?
What pomegranate raised you from the dead,
Springing, full-grown, from your own head, Athena?

I will speak about women of letters, for I'm in the racket

I will speak about women of letters, for I'm in the racket.
Our biggest successes to date? Old maids to a woman.
And our saddest conspicuous failures? The married
        spinsters
On loan to the husbands they treated like surrogate fathers.
Think of that crew of self-pitiers, not-very-distant,
Who carried the torch for themselves and got first-degree
        burns.
Or the sad sonneteers, toast-and-teasdales we loved at
        thirteen;
Middle-aged virgins seducing the puerile anthologists
Through lust-of-the-mind; barbiturate-drenched Camilles
With continuous periods, murmuring softly on sofas
When poetry wasn't a craft but a sickly effluvium,
The air thick with incense, musk, and emotional blackmail.

I suppose they reacted from an earlier womanly modesty
When too many girls were scabs to their stricken
        sisterhood,
Impugning our sex to stay in good with the men,
Commencing their insecure bluster. How they must have
        swaggered

118

When women themselves indorsed their own inferiority!
Vestals, vassals and vessels, rolled into several,
They took notes in rolling syllabics, in careful journals,
Aiming to please a posterity that despises them.
But we'll always have traitors who swear that a woman
      surrenders
Her Supreme Function, by equating Art with aggression
And failure with Femininity. Still, it's just as unfair
To equate Art with Femininity, like a prettily-packaged
      commodity
When we are the custodians of the world's best-kept secret:
Merely the private lives of one-half of humanity.

But even with masculine dominance, we mares and mistresses
Produced some sleek saboteuses, making their cracks
Which the porridge-brained males of the day were too
      thick to perceive,
Mistaking young hornets for perfectly harmless bumblebees.
Being thought innocuous rouses some women to frenzy;
They try to be ugly by aping the ways of the men
And succeed. Swearing, sucking cigars and scorching the
      bedspread,
Slopping straight shots, eyes blotted, vanity-blown
In the expectation of glory: *she writes like a man!*
This drives other women mad in a mist of chiffon
(one poetess draped her gauze over red flannels, a practical
      feminist).

But we're emerging from all that, more or less,
Except for some lady-like laggards and Quarterly priestesses
Who flog men for fun, and kick women to maim competition.
Now, if we struggle abnormally, we may almost seem normal;
If we submerge our self-pity in disciplined industry;
If we stand up and be hated, and swear not to sleep with
      editors;
If we regard ourselves formally, respecting our true limitations
Without making an unseemly show of trying to unfreeze our
      assets;

119

Keeping our heads and our pride while remaining unmarried;
And if wedded, kill guilt in its tracks when we stack up the
    dishes
And defect to the typewriter. And if mothers, believe in the
    luck of our children,
Whom we forbid to devour us, whom we shall not devour,
And the luck of our husbands and lovers, who keep
    free women.

85

36 *pomegranate*: in Greek myth, the food of the dead. Persephone, because
she ate four pomegranate seeds given her by Pluto, king of Hades, was
obliged to dwell with him four months of each year. 37 *Springing* . . .
Athena: Athena, Greek goddess of wisdom, was born fully grown from the
forehead of Zeus. 44 *toast-and-teasdales*: Sara Teasdale (1884–1933),
American poet noted for delicate, crafted love lyrics. In T. S. Eliot's poem
"The Love Song of J. Alfred Prufrock," the taking of toast and tea is a
ritual of a sophisticated, but desiccated, society. 46 *Camilles*: Camille,
heroine of a play of the same name by Alexandre Dumas the younger: a pale,
delicate beauty who dies of tuberculosis.

Hypocrite Women

Hypocrite women, how seldom we speak
of our own doubts, while dubiously
we mother man in his doubt!

And if at Mill Valley perched in the trees
the sweet rain drifting through western air
a white sweating bull of a poet told us

our cunts are ugly — why didn't we
admit we have thought so too? (And
what shame? They are not for the eye!)

No, they are dark and wrinkled and hairy,
caves of the Moon . . .   And when a
dark humming fills us, a

coldness towards life,
we are too much women to
own to such unwomanliness.

Whorishly with the psychopomp
we play and plead — and say
nothing of this later.   And our dreams,

with what frivolity we have pared them
like toenails, clipped them like ends of
split hair.

121

Sister Pharaoh

Hatshepsut, old girl, old friend,
man-woman, bearded Pharaoh,
we women too pasted on beards
and said we were kings.
We brought lullaby rules of commerce to the state,
we raised temples and wrote hieroglyphs
and got the men
to erect an obelisk for us.

Hatshepsut,
you crouch in the silent hall of tombs,
trying to be a riddle.
But we can see through your beard.
Beneath your terrible crown of upper and lower Egypt,
beneath your archaic stone smile,
our milk has turned to powder,
our breasts are two inches of dust.

I am the only being whose doom

I am the only being whose doom
No tongue would ask, no eye would mourn;
I never caused a thought of gloom,
A smile of joy, since I was born.

In secret pleasure, secret tears,
This changeful life has slipped away:
As friendless after eighteen years,
As lone as on my natal day.

There have been times I cannot hide,
There have been times when this was drear,
When my sad soul forgot its pride
And longed for one to love me here.

But those were in the early glow
Of feelings since subdued by care;
And they have died so long ago,
I hardly now believe they were.

First melted off the hope of youth,
Then fancy's rainbow fast withdrew;
And then experience told me truth
In mortal bosoms never grew.

'Twas grief enough to think mankind
All hollow, servile, insincere,
But worse to trust to my own mind
And find the same corruption there.

The Applicant

First, are you our sort of a person?
Do you wear
A glass eye, false teeth or a crutch,
A brace or a hook,
Rubber breasts or a rubber crotch,

Stitches to show something's missing? No, no? Then
How can we give you a thing?
Stop crying.
Open your hand.
Empty? Empty. Here is a hand

To fill it and willing
To bring teacups and roll away headaches
And do whatever you tell it.
Will you marry it?
It is guaranteed

To thumb shut your eyes at the end
And dissolve of sorrow.
We make new stock from the salt.
I notice you are stark naked.
How about this suit ——

Black and stiff, but not a bad fit.
Will you marry it?
It is waterproof, shatterproof, proof
Against fire and bombs through the roof.
Believe me, they'll bury you in it.

Now your head, excuse me, is empty.
I have the ticket for that.
Come here, sweetie, out of the closet.
Well, what do you think of *that?*
Naked as paper to start

But in twenty-five years she'll be silver,
In fifty, gold.
A living doll, everywhere you look.
It can sew, it can cook,
35   It can talk, talk, talk.

It works, there is nothing wrong with it.
You have a hole, it's a poultice.
You have an eye, it's an image.
My boy, it's your last resort.
40   Will you marry it, marry it, marry it.

My Last Duchess

FERRARA

That's my last Duchess painted on the wall,
Looking as if she were alive. I call
That piece a wonder, now; Frà Pandolf's hands
Worked busily a day, and there she stands.
Will 't please you sit and look at her? I said
"Frà Pandolf" by design, for never read
Strangers like you that pictured countenance,
The depth and passion of its earnest glance,
But to myself they turned (since none puts by
The curtain I have drawn for you, but I)
And seemed as they would ask me, if they durst,
How such a glance came there; so, not the first
Are you to turn and ask thus. Sir, 'twas not
Her husband's presence only, called that spot
Of joy into the Duchess' cheek; perhaps
Frà Pandolf chanced to say, "Her mantle laps
Over my lady's wrist too much," or "Paint
Must never hope to reproduce the faint
Half-flush that dies along her throat." Such stuff
Was courtesy, she thought, and cause enough
For calling up that spot of joy. She had
A heart — how shall I say? — too soon made glad,
Too easily impressed; she liked whate'er
She looked on, and her looks went everywhere.
Sir, 'twas all one! My favor at her breast,
The dropping of the daylight in the West,
The bough of cherries some officious fool
Broke in the orchard for her, the white mule
She rode with round the terrace — all and each
Would draw from her alike the approving speech,
Or blush, at least. She thanked men, — good! but thanked
Somehow — I know not how — as if she ranked
My gift of a nine-hundred-years' old name
With anybody's gift. Who'd stoop to blame
This sort of trifling? Even had you skill

In speech — which I have not — to make your will
Quite clear to such an one, and say, "Just this
Or that in you disgusts me; here you miss,
Or there exceed the mark" — and if she let
40   Herself be lessoned so, nor plainly set
Her wits to yours, forsooth, and made excuse —
E'en then would be some stooping; and I choose
Never to stoop. Oh, sir, she smiled, no doubt,
Whene'er I passed her; but who passed without
45   Much the same smile? This grew; I gave commands;
Then all smiles stopped together. There she stands
As if alive. Will 't please you rise? We'll meet
The company below, then. I repeat,
The Count your master's known munificence
50   Is ample warrant that no just pretense
Of mine for dowry will be disallowed;
Though his fair daughter's self, as I avowed
At starting, is my object. Nay, we'll go
Together down, sir. Notice Neptune, though,
55   Taming a sea-horse, thought a rarity,
Which Claus of Innsbruck cast in bronze for me!

Ferrara, a city in northern Italy, is the scene. The speaker may have been
modeled after Alonzo, Duke of Ferrara (1533–1598). 3 *Frà Pandolf* and
56 *Claus of Innsbruck:* fictitious names of artists.

The Housewife's Lament

One day I was walking, I heard a complaining,
And saw an old woman the picture of gloom.
She gazed at the mud on her doorstep ('twas raining)
And this was her song as she wielded her broom.

Chorus:

Oh, life is a toil and love is a trouble,
Beauty will fade and riches will flee,
Pleasures they dwindle and prices they double,
And nothing is as I would wish it to be.

There's too much of worriment goes to a bonnet,
There's too much of ironing goes to a shirt,
There's nothing that pays for the time you waste on it,
There's nothing that lasts us but trouble and dirt.

In March it is mud, it is slush in December,
The midsummer breezes are loaded with dust,
In fall the leaves litter, in muddy September
The wallpaper rots and the candlesticks rust.

There are worms on the cherries and slugs on the roses,
And ants in the sugar and mice in the pies,
The rubbish of spiders no mortal supposes
And ravaging roaches and damaging flies.

With grease and with grime from corner to centre,
Forever at war and forever alert,
No rest for a day lest the enemy enter,
I spend my whole life in a struggle with dirt.

Last night in my dreams I was stationed forever
On a far little rock in the midst of the sea,
My one chance of life was a ceaseless endeavor
To sweep off the waves as they swept over me.

128

Alas! 'Twas no dream; ahead I behold it,
30   I see I am helpless my fate to avert. —
She lay down her broom, her apron she folded,
She lay down and died and was buried in dirt.

"Mrs. Sara A. Price of Ottawa, Illinois, who lost sons in the Civil War, recorded this song of feminine protest in her diary" (Alan Lomax, *Folk Songs of North America*).

129

Before the Birth of
One of Her Children

All things within this fading world hath end,
Adversity doth still our joys attend;
No ties so strong, no friends so dear and sweet,
But with death's parting blow is sure to meet.
5 The sentence past is most irrevocable,
A common thing, yet oh, inevitable.
How soon, my dear, death may my steps attend,
How soon 't may be thy lot to lose thy friend
We both are ignorant; yet love bids me
10 These farewell lines to recommend to thee,
That when that knot's untied that made us one,
I may seem thine, who in effect am none.
And if I see not half my days that's due,
What nature would, God grant to yours and you;
15 The many faults that well you know I have,
Let be interred in my oblivion's grave;
If any worth or virtue were in me,
Let that live freshly in thy memory;
And when thou feel'st no grief, as I no harms,
20 Yet love thy dead, who long lay in thine arms.
And when thy loss shall be repaid with gains,
Look to my little babes, my dear remains.
And if thou love thyself, or loved'st me,
These O protect from stepdame's injury.
25 And if chance to thine eyes shall bring this verse,
With some sad sighs honor my absent hearse;
And kiss this paper for thy love's dear sake,
Who with salt tears this last farewell did take.

The Abortion

Somebody who should have been born
is gone.

Just as the earth puckered its mouth,
each bud puffing out from its knot,
I changed my shoes, and then drove south.

Up past the Blue Mountains, where
Pennsylvania humps on endlessly,
wearing, like a crayoned cat, its green hair,

its roads sunken in like a gray washboard;
where, in truth, the ground cracks evilly,
a dark socket from which the coal has poured,

Somebody who should have been born
is gone.

the grass as bristly and stout as chives,
and me wondering when the ground would break,
and me wondering how anything fragile survives;

up in Pennsylvania, I met a little man,
not Rumpelstiltskin, at all, at all . . .
he took the fullness that love began.

Returning north, even the sky grew thin
like a high window looking nowhere.
The road was as flat as a sheet of tin.

Somebody who should have been born
is gone.

Yes, woman, such logic will lead
to loss without death. Or say what you meant,
you coward . . . this baby that I bleed.

131

The New York Woman

The assistant editor of *Crewel World*
(The Needleworker's Helper, ABC
Paid circulation, 1-1-68,
1,007,773)
Heads home to lunch. In the diffusing lens
Of distance, her long face is pretty, young,
Unfingermarked; close up, it's pretty young,
But hatched with all the crosses of New York:
Divorce, childbearing, wishing, failing, work.
Beside her blue side, her small hand hangs on
To an enormous, tatty orange man's
Briefcase replete with fancyworkers' dreams:
Patterns, instructions, yarn lists, letters, schemes
Of art-struck readers to diffuse their cause
Across the country in a crewel crusade
To mend a ravelled world they never made.
Obliquely, Sarah stares into the dark
Inside her letter box and sees the light-
Er darkness of a letter. Hell, a bill.
Up marble treads she trudges, up until
A skylight drops a halo on her blond,
Untidy head. Palming a porcupine
Of bristling keys, she punctuates the stale
Air of the landing with a yielding Yale-
Lock cluck, and enters into 2 1/2
Rms, rec redec, with fp, kit, and bth.
Her sad son's photo stares, reproaching her,
From grandma's farm above the gas-log fire;
The kitten, claws locked in an afghan, sleeps;
Her pink Picasso juggler mirrors her
Tight lines around the lips. She sighs and goes
To her Rollator-Top GE, which holds
Cat food, pork chops, a wizened chicken leg.
She eats the chicken cold and sips a cup
Of Instant Yuban. Hope, proceeding up
From her warm belly, lodges in her throat
And complicates her swallowing. She tries

A smile extravagantly on for size
And prudently foregoes it. The doorbell
We all sit tight for, powered by a dry cell,
Gives a cracked rattle, and she buzzes in
Her visitor, the editor of *Man*,
Not, as you might suppose, a sword in tan
And turtleneck, but quite instead a pale,
High-foreheaded, mild, intellectual-
Appearing, troubled mother's son named John.
And, judging from his step, he's drunk again.
He swoops in on the door — got it in one —
And espaliers her upon the whitewashed wall
In a facsimile of an embrace
Remembered from bad movies. Find her face
John, and you'll be home free. Shook up, she smiles —
For real this time, like a Madonna does —
And softly scores him for his naughtiness.
He's all for bed; she's all for holding him
Off at arm's length, in her apartment's power,
And owning him with her eyes for an hour,
Until he charges out or falls asleep
On the rag rug beside the kitten's dish.
He falls asleep, as advertised by his
Stertorous radamacues. She gets her wish:
To skip her office afternoon and sit
In silence with another whose needs fit
Her pitiful and unsolicited
Gifts: doglike love, unlimited belief
In journeys' endings, tolerance for grief,
An aptitude for mothering, an art
As painstaking as any crewel heart.

Four Women

My skin is black, my arms are long
My hair is wooly, my back is strong
Strong enough to take the pain
Inflicted again and again,
5   What do they call me? They call me "Aunt Sarah."

My skin is yellow, my hair is long
Between two worlds I do belong
My father was rich and white
He forced my mother late one night,
10   What do they call me? My name is "Safronia."

My skin is tan, my hair is fine
My hips invite you, my mouth like wine
Whose little girl am I
Anyone who has money to buy,
15   What do they call me? My name is "Sweet Thing."

My skin is brown, my manner is tough
I'll kill the first mother I see, my life has been rough
I'm awfully bitter these days
Because my parents were slaves,
20   What do they call me? My name is "Peaches."

Wedding-Wind

The wind blew all my wedding-day,
And my wedding-night was the night of the high wind;
And a stable door was banging, again and again,
That he must go and shut it, leaving me
Stupid in candlelight, hearing rain,
Seeing my face in the twisted candlestick,
Yet seeing nothing. When he came back
He said the horses were restless, and I was sad
That any man or beast that night should lack
The happiness I had.

                    Now in the day
All's ravelled under the sun by the wind's blowing.
He has gone to look at the floods, and I
Carry a chipped pail to the chicken-run,
Set it down, and stare. All is the wind
Hunting through clouds and forests, thrashing
My apron and the hanging cloths on the line.
Can it be borne, this bodying-forth by wind
Of joy my actions turn on, like a thread
Carrying beads? Shall I be let to sleep
Now this perpetual morning shares my bed?
Can even death dry up
These new delighted lakes, conclude
Our kneeling as cattle by all-generous waters?

Morning Has No House

Mornings everything is grey
as in cheap catalogues
reluctant we brush off the rim
of hairy dark you turn
to see whom you've married
I measure my impossible
expectations
gestures hang in the air
exhausted prematurely
my fear of being a kite among winds
your fear I've eaten tigers
in my dreams
but we don't tell about these things
we keep them down
in the body
you rub my arm
erasing the night evidence

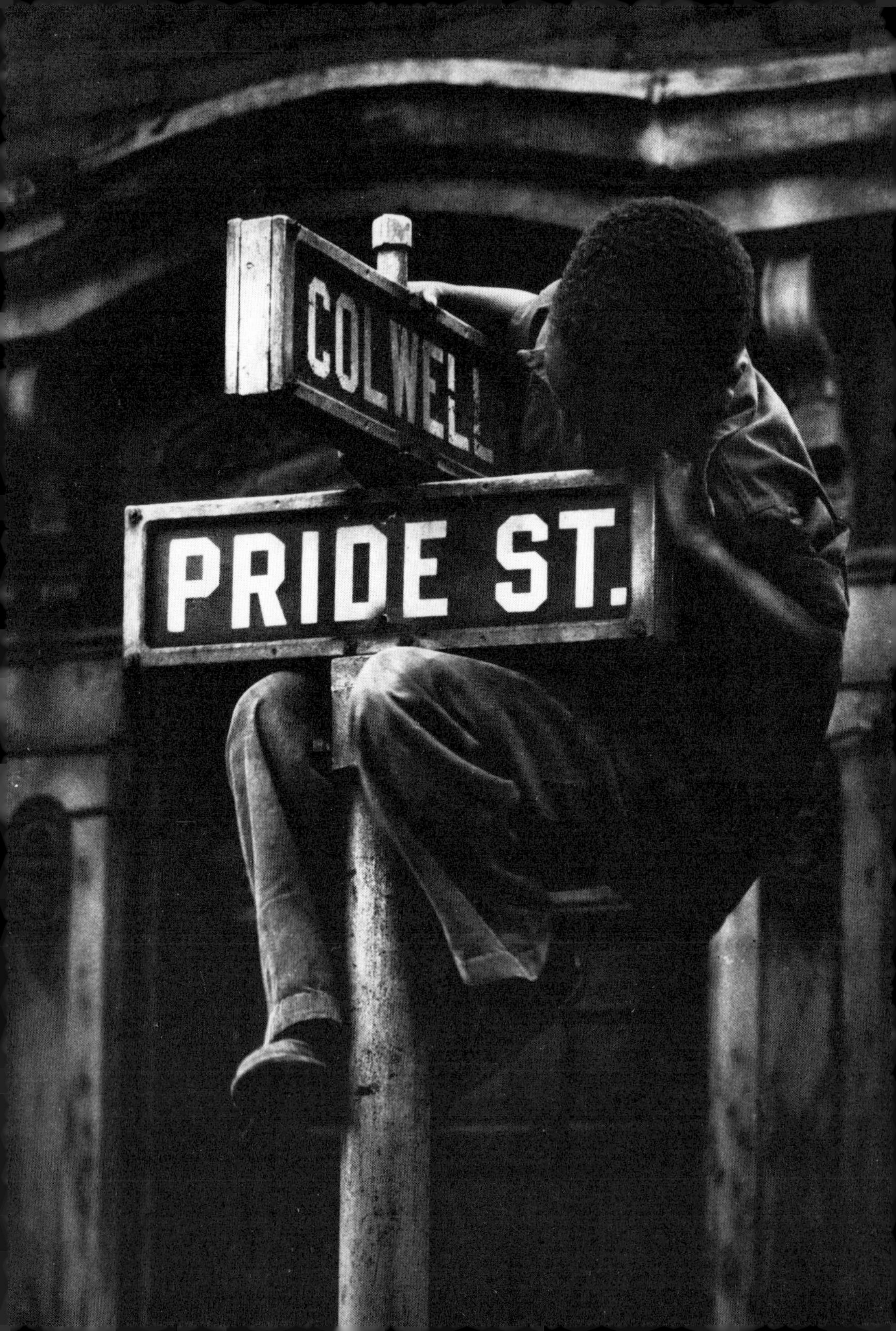
COLWEL
PRIDE ST.

6. The Image in the River

Peoples

No Images

She does not know
Her beauty,
She thinks her brown body
Has no glory.

5 If she could dance
Naked,
Under palm trees
And see her image in the river
She would know.

10 But there are no palm trees
On the street,
And dishwater gives back no images.

O. T.'s Blues

Uncle sent for O. T. told him we have to fight,
Uncle sent for O. T. told him we have to fight,
O. T. caught the huns in a French forest one night.

Sun came up O. T. was dead dead huns all around,
Sun came up O. T. was dead dead huns all around,
Machine gun was still hot he was cold on the ground.

When word came back home how brave black O. T. had died,
When word came back home how brave black O. T. had died,
Well his wife and his mother naturally cried.

The Chocolate Soldiers

Where's the winning without chocolate
I asked the General when the white bombs

Landed on Venus beach and the natives
Shot their tongues into our ears. Once

Chocolate was in front, and strangers
Bit what our hand extended; not laying

Us but we laying them in the dungy hay.
Brown candy melted in colonial mouths

When chocolate was sweet politics; white
Sons wrote home about Guam and bodies

With nude ankles. Now natives lay waste.
The brown will dominate even on Venus beach.

Though I want to admit to taking my mirror
To insure courageous chocolate dwells there.

indian school

in the darkness
of the house of the white brother
i go alone and am frightened
strange things touch me
5   i cannot breathe his air
or eat his tasteless food

on his walls
are pictures of the world
that his walls shut out
10   in his hands are leaves of words
from dead mens mouths

he speaks to me with only
the sounds of his mouth
for he is dumb and blind
15   as the staggering old bear
filled with many arrows
as the rocks that lie on the mountain

and in his odd robes
uglier
20   than any other creature i have ever seen

i am not wise enough to know
gods purpose in him.

Christmas Comes to Moccasin Flat

Christmas comes like this: Wise men
unhurried, candles bought on credit (poor price
for calves), warriors face down in wine sleep.
Winds cheat to pull heat from smoke.

5   Friends sit in chinked cabins, stare out
plastic windows and wait for commodities.
Charley Blackbird, twenty miles from church
and bar, stabs his fire with flint.

When drunks drain radiators for love
10   or need, chiefs eat snow and talk of change,
an urge to laugh pounding their ribs.
Elk play games in high country.

Medicine Woman, clay pipe and twist tobacco,
calls each blizzard by name and predicts
15   five o'clock by spitting at her television.
Children lean into her breath to beg a story:

Something about honor and passion,
warriors back with meat and song,
a peculiar evening star, quick vision of birth.
20   Blackbird builds his fire. Outside, a quick thirty below.

145

Ballad of Ira Hayes

Call him drunken Ira Hayes, he won't answer any more;
Not the whiskey drinkin' Indian, nor the marine that went
    to war.

Gather 'round me, people, and a story I will tell
About a brave young Indian you should remember well,
From the tribe of Pima Indians, the proud and peaceful band,
Who farmed the Phoenix Valley in Arizona land.

Down their ditches for a thousand years that sparklin' water
    rushed
Till the white man stole the water rights and the runnin' water
    hushed.
Now Ira's folks were hungry and their farm grew crops of
    weeds.
When war came Ira volunteered and forgot the white man's
    greed.

Call him drunken Ira Hayes, he won't answer any more;
Not the whiskey drinkin' Indian, nor the marine that went
    to war.

Well, they started up Iwo Jima Hill — two hundred and
    fifty men,
But only twenty-seven men lived — to walk back down again;
And when that fight was over — and Old Glory raised,
Among the men who held it high was the Indian — Ira Hayes.

Call him drunken Ira Hayes, he won't answer any more;
Not the whiskey drinkin' Indian, nor the marine that went
    to war.

Ira Hayes returned a hero — celebrated through this land,
He was wined and speeched and honored, and everybody shook
    his hand;
But he was just a Pima Indian — no water, no crops, no chance;
At home nobody cared what Ira done — and when do the
    Indians dance?

146

Call him drunken Ira Hayes, he won't answer any more;
Not the whiskey drinkin' Indian, nor the marine that went
    to war.

25   Then Ira started drinkin' hard — jail often was his home;
They let him raise the flag there, and lower it — as you'd
    throw a dog a bone.
He died drunk early one morning — alone in this land he'd
    fought to save;
Two inches of water in a lonely ditch was the grave for Ira Hayes.

Call him drunken Ira Hayes, he won't answer any more;
Not the whiskey drinkin' Indian, nor the marine that went
30   to war.

Yes, call him drunken Ira Hayes — but his lands they're still
    as dry,
And his ghost is a-lyin' thirsty in the ditch where Ira died.

Spontaneous Requiem for the American Indian

Wakonda! Talako! deathonic turkey gobbling in the soft-
        footpatch night!
Blue-tipped yellow-tipped red-tipped feathers of whort dye
        fluffing in fire mad dance whaa whaa dead men red
        men feathers-in-their-head-men night!
Deerskin rage of flesh on the bone on the hot tobacco ground!
Muskhogean requiems america southeastern, O death of
        Creeks, Choctaws,
5   The youthful tearful Brave, in his dying hand trout, well-
        caught proud trout,
Softest of feet, fleet, o america dirge, o america norwegians
        swedes of quid and murder and boots and slaughter
        and God and rot-letters,
O pinto brays! O deatheme sled mourning the dying chief!
Berries, spruce, whortle, cranky corn, bitter wheat; o scarcity
        of men!
High-throttled squawlark, sister warrior, teepee maid, scar
        lover, crash down thy muskrat no longer thy flesh
        hand and rage and writhe and pound thy Indianic
        earth with last pang of love of love,
10   o america, o requiems —

Ghost-herds of uneaten left to rot animals thundering across
        the plains
Chasing the ghost of England across the plains forever ever,
        pompous Kiwago raging in the still Dakotas, o america —
America o mineral scant america o mineralize america o
        conferva of that once
great lovely Muskhogean pool, o oil-suck america despite,
        oil from forgetive days, hare to arrow, muskellunge to
        spear, fleet-footed know ye speed-well the tribes
        thence outraced the earth to eat to love to die,
15   o requiems, Hathor off-far bespeaks Wakonda,
heraldic henequen tubas whittled in coyote tune to mourn
        the death of the going sun the going sled of each
        dying, sad and dying, shake of man, the tremble of

men, of each dying chief slow and red and leather
fur hot —
Shake slow the rattler, the hawk-teeth, the bettle-bells,
shake slow dirge, o dirge, shake slow the winds of
winds, o feathers withered and blown,
Dirge the final pinto-led sled, the confused hurt sad king of
Montanas,
Strike dumb the French fur trappers in their riverboat brool
mockery, no chant of death in such a wealth of musk-
rat and beaver, shun them,
O slam squaw hysteria down on america, the covered wagon
america, the arrow flamed wagons of conquest, the
death stand of quakers and white-hooded hags and
proud new men, young and dead,
O Geronimo! hard nickel faced Washington Boliva of a
dying city that never was, that monster-died, that
demons gathered to steal and did,
O Sitting Bull! pruneman Jefferson Lenin Lincoln reddead
man, force thy spirit to wings, cloud the earth to air,
o the condor the vulture the hawk fat days are gone,
and you are gone, o america, o requiems,
Dry valleys, deathhead stones, high Arizonas, red sun earth,
the sled,
The weeping bray, the ponymarenight, the slow chief of
death, wrinkled and sad and manless, vistaless, smoke-
less, proud sad dying —
Toward the coyote reach of peak and moon, howl of hey-
day, laugh proud of men and men, Blackfoot, Mo-
hawk, Algonquin, Seneca, all men, o american, peaked
there then bow
Thy white-haired straw head and, pinto imitated, die with
the rising moon, hotnight, lost, empty, unseen, music-
less, mindless; no wind —
In the grim dread light of the Happy Hunting Ground
A century of chiefs argue their many scalps, whacking the yellow
strands of a child against the coaly misty harsh of tent;

It falls apart in a scatter of strewn, away, gone, no more,
 back free out of the quay, into the bladder seep of
 the bald dead seeking the hairless rawhead child of
 whiteman's grave;

O there is more an exact sorrow in this Indianical eternity,
Sure o america woof and haw and caw and wooooo whirl
 awhirl here o weep!
Indianhill woe! never was the scalp of men the prime knife
 in the heart of a savagengence era, Clevelandestroyer
 of manland, o requiems,
O thundercloud, thunderbird, rain-in-the-face, hark in the
 gloom, death,
And blankets and corn, and peaceful footings of man in
 quest of Kiwago, america, Kiwago, america, corn
 america, earthly song of a sad boy's redfleshed song
 in the night before the peered head intrusive head of
 laughing thunderbolt Zeus, o the prank, o the death,
 o the night,
Requiem, america, sing a dirge that might stalk the white
 wheat black in praise of Indianever again to be, gone,

 gone, desolate, and gone;
Hear the plains, the great divide, here the wind of this night
 Oklahoma race to weep first in the dirge of mountains and
 streams and trees and birds and day and night and the
 bright yet lost apparitional sled,
The bowed head of an Indian is enough to bow the horse's
 head and both in unison die and die and die, and never
 again die for once the night eats up the dying it eats up the
 pain and there is no Indian pain no pregnant squaw no
 wild-footed great-eyed boy no jolly stern fat white-furred
 chief of tobacco damp and sweet, o america america —
Each year Kiwago must watch its calves thin out; must
 watch with all its natural killers dead, the new
 marksmen of machines and bullets and trained studied
 eyes aim and fire and kill the oldest bull, the king, the
 Kiwago of the reminiscent plain —

Each year Wakonda must watch the motionless desert, the
     dry tearless childless desert, the smokeless desert, the
     Indianlessadly desert —
Each year Talako must watch the bird go arrowless in his
     peace of sky in his freedom of the mouth of old america,
     raw wild calm america,
O america, o requiem, o tumbleweed, o Western Sky, each
     year is another year the soft football doesn't fall, the
     thin strong arm of spear never raised, the wise council
     of gathered kings no longer warm with life and fur and
     damp and heat and hotcorn and dry jerky meat, each year
     no squaw titters her moony lover of hard love and
     necessary need of man and wife and child child, each
     year no child, no mien of life, good life, no, no, america,
     but the dead stones, the dry trees, the dusty going
     winded earth — requiem.

Pilgrim blunderbuss, buckles, high hat, Dutch, English, pat-
ent leather shoes, Bible, pray, snow, careful, careful, o but
feast, turkey, corn, pumpkin, sweet confused happy hosty
guests, Iroquois, Mohawk, Oneida, Onondaga, Thanksgiving!
O joy! o angels! o peace! o land! land land land,
     o death,
O fire and arrow and buckshot and whisky and rum and
     death and land,
O witches and taverns and quakers and Salem and New
     Amsterdam and corn,
And night, softfeet, death, massacre, massacre, o america,
     o requiem —
Log-cabins, forts, outposts, trading-posts, in the distance, clouds,
Dust, hordes, tribes, death, death, blonde girls to die, gowns
     of ladies to burn, men of redcoats and bluecoats to
     die, boys to drum and fife and curse and cry and die,
     horses . . . to die, babies . . . to die;
Yeeeeeeeeeeeeeeeooooooooooo! Harrrrrrrrrrrrrrraaaaaaaaaa!
EEEEEEEEeeeeeeEEEEEEaaaaaaaaaaaaah!

To die to die to die to die to die to die . . . america, requiem.
Corn, jerky, whortly, the Seneca in a deacon's suit, gawky,
55   awkward, drunk,
Tired, slouched — the gowns and bright boots pass, the quick
take-your-partner-swing-to-the-left-swing-to-the-right hums
all is over, done, the Seneca sleeps, no sled, no pinto, no end,
but sleep, and a new era, a new day, a new light and the
60   corn grows plenty, and the night is forever, and the day;

The jetliner streams down upon Texas,
                    Requiem.

Motorcyclist Blackfoot his studded belt at night wilder than
bright hawkeyes sits on his fat bike black smelly brusqued
65   assy about to goggleeye himself down golden ventures whiz-
zing faster than his ancestral steed past smokestacks banner-
shacks O the timid shade of Kiwago now! the mad roar
exhaustpipe Indian like a fleeing over clanking weeeeee
weeeeeee no feathers in his oily helmet O he's a fast engine
70   of steam zooming unlaurelled by but he's stupid he sits in
Horn & Hardart's his New York visit and he's happy with
his short girls with pink faces and bright hair talking about
his big fat bike and their big fat bike, O he's an angel there
though sinister sinister in shape of Steel Discipline smoking
75   a cigarette in a fishy corner in the night, waiting, america,
waiting the end, the last Indian, mad Indian of no fish or
foot or proud forest haunt, mad on his knees ponytailing &
rabbitfooting his motorcycle, his the final requiem the final
america READY THE FUNERAL STOMP goodluck charms
80   on, tires aired, spikes greased, morose goggles on, motor gas
brakes checked! 1958 Indians, heaps of leather — ZOOM
down the wide amber speedway of Death, Little Richard,
tuba mirum, the vast black jacket brays in the full forced fell.

In the Jury Room

Grinning, the foreman asked them for a vote,
A formal act, and one to deprecate.
They'd sat all day; they musn't leave too late
For loafing, when their verdict noosed a throat.
Plain murder; Hell, the trial wasted time . . .
But Hendrix didn't hold so. Their debate
Dinned in his ears. *Why Christ, man, at this rate*
If niggers kill a white man, 'tain't a crime!

And you'd have killed him, too, he said. They jeered,
And almost cut away the jerking ghost
Suspended in his mind. But though he feared
The dangling wraith, he feared his neighbors most.
So, swallowing hard against the choking foam,
"All right," he said, "he's guilty — let's go home."

Why I Sing the Blues

Everybody wants to know why I sing the blues
Yes, I say everybody wants to know why I sing the blues
Well, I've been around a long time, I really have paid my dues.

When I first got the blues, they brought me over on a ship
Men was standing over me and a lot more with the whip
And everybody wanna know why I sing the blues
Well I've been around a long time, uum, I really paid my dues.

Laid in the Ghetto Flats cold and numb
I heard the rats tell the bedbugs to give the roaches some
And everybody wanna know why I sing the blues
We'll I've been around a long time, uum, I really paid my dues.

Stood in line down in the County Hall
I heard a man say we are going to build some new apartments
       for y'all
And everybody wanna know why I sing the blues
Well I've been around a long time, uum, I really paid my dues.

My kid's gonna grow up, gonna grow up to be a fool
'Cause they ain't got no more room, no more room for him
       in school
And everybody want to know why I sing the blues
I say I've been around a long time, yes I have really paid my dues.

Yea, you know the company told me, yes, you're born to lose
Everybody around feel it, seem like everybody's got the blues
But I had them a long time, I really, really paid my dues
You know I ain't ashamed of it, people, I just love to sing
       the blues.

I walk through the city, people, on my bare feet,
I had a fill of catfish and chitlins up and down Beale Street.
You know I'm singin' the blues, yes, I really just have to sing
       my blues.
I've been around a long time, people, I really, really paid my
       dues.

Now, father time is catching up with me, and so is my youth,
I look in the mirror ev'ry day and let it tell me the truth.
I'm singing the blues, um, um, um, I just have to sing the blues.
I've been around a long time, um, um, I really paid my dues.

Yes, they told me ev'rything would be better up the country,
Um, ev'rything was fine. I caught me a bus up town, baby,
And all the people got the same trouble as mine.
I got the blues ———— uh, huh!
I've been around a long time, um, um, I really paid some dues.

Blind man on the corner, beggin' for a dime.
The roller come and caught him and threw him in the jail
        for a crime,
I got the blues. ———— um, um, I'm singin' my blues,
I've been around a long time, um, I really paid some dues.

Stagolee

It was early Sunday mornin
When I heard my bulldog bark.
Stagolee and Billy Lyons
Was squabblin in the dark.

5   Stagolee told Billy Lyons,
"Can't let you go with that.
You win all my money, Billy,
And my milk-white Stetson hat."

Stagolee he went out walkin
10   In the red-hot broilin sun.
"Look in my bureau drawer, Alberta,
Hand me my smokeless 41."

Stagolee he took out his Elgin,
Looked directly at the time.
15   "I got an argument to settle
With that weasel Billy Lyons."

Billy Lyons started to holler,
"Stag, please don't take my life,
I got three little helpless babies
20   And one poor pitiful wife."

"Don't care nothin bout your children,
Don't care nothin bout your wife.
You done mistreated me, Billy,
So I'm bound to take your life."

25   Stag shot him three times in the forehead,
Shot him three times in the right side.
"Gonna keep on shootin, Billy,
Till you gone and died."

Stagolee told Mrs. Billy,
30   "Don't you believe your man is dead?
Come into the bar-room,
See the hole I shot through his head."

Mrs. Billy fell to her knee-caps,
Say to her tallest son,
35 "Just you get a little bit bigger,
Gonna buy you a 41."

"Momma, O momma, momma,
You sure ain't talkin to me.
He killed my poor old daddy,
40 Now you about to make him kill me."

Chief Maloney told the deputies,
"Get your pistols and come with me.
We got to go arrest that
Bad man Stagolee."

45 Deputies took off their white tin badges,
Slowly laid them on the shelf.
"If you want that bad man Stagolee,
Go arrest him your own self."

Chief Maloney said to the bartender,
50 "Who might that sleeping man be?"
"Speak softly," said the bartender,
"It's that bad man Stagolee."

He touch Stag on the shoulder,
"Stag, why don't you run?" —
55 "I don't run, white folks,
When I got my 41."

Stagolee he tried to get up,
Couldn't get his 41 out.
Chief Maloney pulled his pistol,
60 Shot the poor boy in the mouth.

The hangman put the mask on,
Tied Stag's hands behind his back,
Sprung the trap on Stagolee,
But his neck refuse to crack.

65 Hangman he got frightened,
"Chief, you see how it be —
I can't hang this bad man,
Better let him go free."

Chief Maloney said to the hangman,
70 "Before I let him go alive —"
He up with his police special,
Shot him six times in the side.

Three hundred dollar funeral,
Thousand dollar hearse,
75 Satisfaction undertaker
Put Stag six feet down in the earth.

Stagolee he told the Devil,
"Come on and have some fun.
You stick me with your pitchfork,
80 I'll shoot you with my 41."

All the Devil's little babies
Run like bedbugs up the wall.
"Catch him, pretty poppa,
Before he kill us all."

85 Stagolee took the pitchfork
And he laid it on the shelf —
"Stand back, Tom Devil,
I'm gonna rule Hell by myself."

Versions of this ballad have multiplied; this one is a composite of several. In some of them Stagolee (or Stackerlee) comes from Memphis, in others from St. Louis. Some versions say that Stagolee's Stetson hat gave him superhuman powers and that he got it by selling his soul to the Devil.

The Metamorphosis of Aunt Jemima

For years she smiled
with her apron white teeth,
a honeydew grin
warming the kitchen of whitefolks' homes.

5   Her face was mellow brown,
because black was not yet beautiful,
and under a knotted kerchief
her hair was frizzed and crisp

and something kids marveled at.
10   Sometimes, after a Steppin Fetchit movie,
Aunt Jemima minded a hot stove,
always smiling,
that we might taste a simpler age.

But I grew up, and had children
15   and breakfasts of my own,
and one day the portrait on the box
was not the same.
The smile was thinner and colder

and the eyes frightened my pale offspring.
20   Still, I brought her home,
for old habits die hard.
And how better could I reward
all her loyalty and kindness?

It's too late to help her now, of course.
25   I only wish I could have foreseen
the dark, congested face,
the upraised hand,
the fist clenched against all
the white tomorrows,
30   the death of pancakes in America.

They Feed They Lion

Out of burlap sacks, out of bearing butter,
Out of black bean and wet slate bread,
Out of the acids of rage, the candor of tar,
Out of cresote, gasoline, drive shafts, wooden dollies
They Lion grow.
                Out of the gray hills
Of industrial barns, out of rain, out of bus ride
West Virginia to Kiss My Ass, out of buried aunties,
Mothers hardening like pounded stumps, out of stumps,
Out of the bones' need to sharpen and the muscles' to stretch,
They Lion grow.
                Earth is eating trees, fence posts,
Gutted cars, earth is calling in her little ones,
"Come home, Come home!" From pig balls,
From the ferocity of pig driven to holiness,
From the furred ear and the full jowl come
The repose of the hung belly, from the purpose
They Lion grow.
                From the sweet glues of the trotters
Come the sweet kinks of the fist, from the full flower
Of the hams the thorax of caves,
From "Bow Down" come "Rise up,"
Come they Lion from the reeds of shovels,
The grained arm that pulls the hands,
They Lion grow.
                From my five arms and all my hands,
From all my white sins forgiven, they feed,
From my car passing under the stars,
They Lion, from my children inherit,
From the oak turned to a wall, they Lion,
From they sack and they belly opened
And all that was hidden burning on the oil-stained earth
They feed they Lion and he comes.

If something should happen

for instance
if the sea should break
and crash against the decks
and below decks break the cargo
against the sides of the sea
or
if the chains should break
and crash against the decks
and below decks break the sides
of the sea
or
if the seas of cities
should crash against each other
and break the chains
and break the walls holding down the cargo
and break the sides of the seas
and all the waters of the earth wash together
in a rush of breaking
where will the captains run and
to what harbor?

7. The End of the World
Nightmare and Apocalypse

The End of the World

Quite unexpectedly as Vasserot
The armless ambidextrian was lighting
A match between his great and second toe,
And Ralph the lion was engaged in biting
5   The neck of Madame Sossman while the drum
Pointed, and Teeny was about to cough
In waltz-time swinging Jocko by the thumb —
Quite unexpectedly the top blew off:

And there, there overhead, there, there hung over
10   Those thousands of white faces, those dazed eyes,
There in the starless dark the poise, the hover,
There in vast wings across the canceled skies,
There in the sudden blackness the black pall
Of nothing, nothing, nothing — nothing at all.

Lady Lazarus

I have done it again.
One year in every ten
I manage it —

A sort of walking miracle, my skin
Bright as a Nazi lampshade,
My right foot

A paperweight,
My face a featureless, fine
Jew linen.

Peel off the napkin
O my enemy.
Do I terrify? —

The nose, the eye pits, the full set of teeth?
The sour breath
Will vanish in a day.

Soon, soon the flesh
The grave cave ate will be
At home on me

And I a smiling woman.
I am only thirty.
And like the cat I have nine times to die.

This is Number Three.
What a trash
To annihilate each decade.

What a million filaments.
The peanut-crunching crowd
Shoves in to see

Them unwrap me hand and foot —
The big strip tease.
Gentleman, ladies,

These are my hands,
My knees.
I may be skin and bone,

166

Nevertheless, I am the same, identical woman.
The first time it happened I was ten.
It was an accident.

The second time I meant
To last it out and not come back at all.
I rocked shut

As a seashell.
They had to call and call
And pick the worms off me like sticky pearls.

Dying
Is an art, like everything else.
I do it exceptionally well.

I do it so it feels like hell.
I do it so it feels real.
I guess you could say I've a call.

It's easy enough to do it in a cell.
It's easy enough to do it and stay put.
It's the theatrical

Comeback in broad day
To the same place, the same face, the same brute
Amused shout:

"A miracle!"
That knocks me out.
There is a charge

For the eyeing of my scars, there is a charge
For the hearing of my heart —
It really goes.

And there is a charge, a very large charge
For a word or a touch
Or a bit of blood

Or a piece of my hair or my clothes.
So, so, Herr Doktor.
So, Herr Enemy.

I am your opus,
I am your valuable,
The pure gold baby

70   That melts to a shriek.
I turn and burn.
Do not think I underestimate your great concern.

Ash, ash —
You poke and stir.
75   Flesh, bone, there is nothing there —

A cake of soap,
A wedding ring,
A gold filling.

Herr God, Herr Lucifer,
80   Beware
Beware.

Out of the ash
I rise with my red hair
And I eat men like air.

Finding the Pistol

Dragging a rake through layers of my sleep
Blown down like leaves in a dream of weather,
I haul to light as through a developing water
Something the child has never seen before,
Though she knows it clearly for a kind of weapon.
It is a snub-nosed pistol, gray and scabbed with rust
The color of blood or the leaves that covered it.
She fondles it and turns it over in her hand
Until I see it batten on her knuckle
Like a damaged finger and she cannot let it go.
She aims it at me out of every bush
And I can hear the hammer clicking like a shutter.
Someone is taking a picture of me.
It comes up smoking through the leaves of water
And smiles down at me from my father's gallery.
I never saw till now the thing I nestled in my hand
And pointed like a finger at the camera.
I never knew before who took the photograph,
Who lost a heartbeat when he heard the hammer fall,
As it will no more than once or twice in our
Overlapping lives, on an empty chamber.

Assassination Poems

Not Believing It

The night is very dark
we see the cars moving
some by their lights
some by the darkening of the dark
5   and some cars moving without lights

Not Wanting to Believe It

That is the name of a far star:
Arcturus, it was written about.
Other stars too
have names, in constellations
10   one by one going out and
being born
"like fireflies in a summer night"

Knowing It

By the stream, squatting,
I try to slice
15   the water with my hands
into blocks, to lift them
into place, liquid blocks of clear water,
on the grass bank

The Assassin

And now we must begin to eat him:
20   we eat his hair, his lips, his eyelids,
his mother and father, his brothers,
his school friends, his buddies, his fiancées,
his minister, his employers, his books.
We eat everything we can find of his past,
25   we eat him in the present until we are stuffed full,
our gullets burning with all we have had to swallow,
guts bloating with the accumulation of his weeks and years.

170

The Friends

They turn to each other quickly
weaving a basket, trying to weave
a basket of words
watertight, greased to hold grief

The Nation

A house united by death
is a house of death

in which death is the head
of the house,

and we do as He says

Kent State, May 4, 1970

Ran out of tear gas and became panicky,
poor inept kids, and therefore they poured lead
into the other kids and shot them dead,
and now myself and the whole country

5   are weeping. It's not a matter of degree,
not less not more than the Indo-Chinese slaughtered,
it is the same; but mostly folk are shattered
by home truths (as I know who lost my boy).

I am not willing to go on this week

10   with business as usual, this month this year
let cars slow down and stop and builders break
off building and close up the theater.
You see, the children that we massacre
are our own children. Call the soldiers back.

Mother the Wardrobe Is Full of Infantrymen

mother the wardrobe is full of infantrymen
i did i asked them
but they snarled saying it was a mans life

mother there is a centurian tank in the parlour
i did i asked the officer
but he laughed saying 'Queens regulations'
(piano was out of tune anyway)

mother polish your identity bracelet
there is a mushroom cloud in the backgarden
i did i tried to bring in the cat
but it simply came to pieces in my hand
i did i tried to whitewash the windows
but there weren't any
i did i tried to hide under the stairs
but i couldn't get in for civil defence leaders
i did i tried ringing candid camera
but they crossed their hearts

i went for a policeman but they were looting the town
i went out for a fire engine but they were all upside down
i went for a priest but they were all on their knees
mother don't just lie there say something please
mother don't just lie there say something please

The Day They Busted the Grateful Dead

The day they busted the Grateful Dead
rain stormed against San Francisco
like hot swampy scissors cutting Justice
into the evil clothes that alligators wear.

The day they busted the Grateful Dead
was like a flight of winged alligators
carefully measuring marble with black
    rubber telescopes.

The day they busted the Grateful Dead
turned like the wet breath of alligators
blowing up balloons the size of the
    Hall of Justice.

174

October and November

1. Che Guevara

Week of Che Guevara, hunted, hurt,
held prisoner one lost day, then gangstered down
for gold, for justice — violence cracking on violence,
rock on rock, the corpse of the last armed prophet
5   laid out on a sink in a shed, revealed by flashlight —
as the leaves light up, still green, this afternoon,
and burn to frittered reds; as the oak, branch-lopped
to go on living, swells with goiters like a fruit-tree,
as the sides of the high white stone buildings over-
10   shadow the poor, too new in the new world,
Manhattan, where our clasped, illicit hands
pulse, stop the bloodstream as if it hit rock. . . .
Rest for the outlaw . . . kings once hid in oaks,
with prices on their heads, and watched for game.

2. Caracas I

15   Through another of our cities without a center, as hideous
as Los Angeles, and with as many cars
per head, and past the 20-foot neon sign
for *Coppertone* on a church, past the population
earning $700 per capita
20   in jerry skyscraper living-slabs, and on to the White House
of El Presidente Leoni, his small men with 18-
inch repeating pistols, firing 45 bullets a minute,
the two armed guards petrified beside us, while we had
        champagne,
and someone bugging the President: 'Where are the girls?'
25   And the enclosed leader, quite a fellow, saying,
'I don't know where yours are, but I know where to find
        mine.' . . .
This house, this pioneer democracy, built
on foundations, not of rock, but blood as hard as rock.

175

3. *The March I*

FOR DWIGHT MACDONALD

Under the too white marmoreal Lincoln Memorial,
the too tall marmoreal Washington Obelisk,
gazing into the too long reflecting pool,
the reddish trees, the withering autumn sky,
the remorseless, amplified harangues for peace —
lovely to lock arms, to march absurdly locked
(unlocking to keep my wet glasses from slipping)
to see the cigarette match quaking in my fingers,
then to step off like green Union Army recruits
for the first Bull Run, sped by photographers,
the notables, the girls . . . fear, glory, chaos, rout . . .
our green army staggered out on the miles-long green fields,
met by the other army, the Martian, the ape, the hero,
his new-fangled rifle, his green new steel helmet.

4. *The March II*

Where two or three were heaped together, or fifty,
mostly white-haired, or bald, or women . . . sadly
unfit to follow their dream, I sat in the sunset
shade of their Bastille, the Pentagon,
nursing leg- and arch-cramps, my cowardly,
foolhardy heart; and heard, alas, more speeches,
though the words took heart now to show how weak
we were, and right. An MP sergeant kept
repeating, 'March slowly through them. Don't even brush
anyone sitting down.' They tiptoed through us
in single file, and then their second wave
trampled us flat and back. Health to those who held,
health to the green steel head . . . to your kind hands
that helped me stagger to my feet, and flee.

5. *Charles Russell Lowell: 1835–1864*

Hard to exhume him from the other Union martyrs;
though common now, his long-short, crisping hair,

176

his green mustache, the manly, foppish coat —
60   more and more often he turns up as a student:
twelve horses killed under him — a nabob cousin
bred, then shipped replacements. He had, *gave* . . . everything
at Cedar Creek — his men dismounted, firing
repeating carbines; heading two vicious charges,
65   the slug collapsing his bad, tubercular lung:
fainting, bleeding, loss of voice above a whisper;
Phil Sheridan — any captain since Joshua — shouting:
'I'll sleep in the enemy camp tonight, or hell. . . .'
Charles had himself strapped to the saddle . . . bound to death,
70   his cavalry that scorned the earth it trod on.

6. Caracas II

With words handled like the new grass writhing, rippling
in an urban brook, greens washed to double greenness —
one could get through life, though mute, with courage
and a merciful heart — two things, and a third thing:
75   humor . . . as the turned-out squatter clings
with amused bravery that takes the form of mercy
to the Old Square in Caracas, his shaky, one-man hovel,
the spoiled baroque cathedral from the age of Drake.
The church has hay in its courtyard; householders own the
        Common —
80   conservatives reduced to conservation:
green things, the well, the school, the writhing grass;
the communist committed to his commune,
artist and office-holder to a claque of less
than fifty souls . . . to each his venomous in-group.

This self-contained section from Lowell's *Notebook* refers in part 1 to the
death of Che Guevara on October 8, 1967. Guevara, revolutionist and
aide to Fidel Castro in Cuba, was apparently killed by Bolivian troops while
leading a band of guerrillas in an attempt to overthrow the Bolivian
government. Parts 3 and 4 refer to the antiwar protest march on the Pentagon
on October 21, 1967.

177

Speech

1

I crouch over my radio
to tune in the President,
thinking how lucky I am
not to own a television.

2

Now the rich, cultivated voice
with its cautious, measured pauses
fills my living room, fills
the wastebasket, the vase
on the mantel, the hurricane
lamps, and even fills
the antique pottery whiskey jug
beside the fireplace, nourishing
the dried flowers I have put in it.

3

"I had a responsibility,"
he says; the phrase pours
from the speaker like molasses,
flows to the rug, spreads
into a black, shining puddle,
slowly expands, covers
the rug with dark sweetness.
It begins to draw flies;
they eat all the syrup
and clamor for more.

4

I can barely hear the speech
above the buzzing of their wings.
But the Commander-in-Chief

has the solution: another
phrase, sweeter, thicker,
blacker, oozes out
30 over my living room floor:
"I have personal reasons
for wanting peace." This is more
than the flies will be able to eat;
they will stay quiet
35 for the rest of the speech.

5

Now, you are thinking, comes
the Good Part, the part
where the syrup proves poisonous
and kills all the flies.
40 My fellow Americans, that
is not at all what happened.
The flies grew fat on the phrases,
grew as large as bullfrogs.

6

They are everywhere in the house,
45 and the syrup continues
to feed and fatten them;
in the pottery whiskey jug,
sprouting new leaves and buds,
even the dried flowers thrive.

7

50 The speech
has been over for weeks now;
they go on eating,
but they stay quiet

and seem peaceful enough.
55   At night, sometimes,
I can hear them
making soft liquid sounds
of contentment.

Voice from Danang

After we had burned on the water a while,
amid the chopper-borne
shouts, flares, and thrashing rope ladders,
we put into quiet, dark rooms.

5 I couldn't touch you through my walls —
my nails screeled into chines.
Why had they bored lights in me like that?

You must have known we were set on sand.
It scratched in our ears
10 like blood leaking in crystals from my veins.
We waited under a noisy sky.

I have been watching my body fall apart —
toes and eyes like loose bearings,
my torch-light prick chases its batteries.

15 They lift us, number us, lift us, shelve us.
Have your ribs jackstrawed?
Once they tipped me up on concrete, my parts
thundered into my skull.

This will go on and on until we get back.
20 We are cool, invoiced cargo.
I last saw you shouting at a fly on a blue ceiling.

If there was confusion then, there is none now.
I had thought that a bag or box
could not keep me in, but this is plainly a cove —
25 white trees, black sand, waves, sun.

Shine, Perishing Republic

While this America settles in the mould of its vulgarity,
    heavily thickening to empire,
And protest, only a bubble in the molten mass, pops
    and sighs out, and the mass hardens,

I sadly smiling remember that the flower fades to make
    fruit, the fruit rots to make earth.
Out of the mother; and through the spring exultances,
    ripeness and decadence; and home to the mother.

You making haste haste on decay: not blameworthy; life
    is good, be it stubbornly long or suddenly
A mortal splendor: meteors are not needed less than
    mountains: shine, perishing republic.

But for my children, I would have them keep their distance
    from the thickening center; corruption
Never has been compulsory, when the cities lie at the
    monster's feet there are left the mountains.

And boys, be in nothing so moderate as in love of man,
    a clever servant, insufferable master.
There is the trap that catches noblest spirits, that caught
    — they say — God, when he walked on earth.

The Fall of Rome

For Cyril Connolly

The piers are pummeled by the waves;
In a lonely field the rain
Lashes an abandoned train;
Outlaws fill the mountain caves.

5   Fantastic grow the evening gowns;
Agents of the Fisc pursue
Absconding tax-defaulters through
The sewers of provincial towns.

Private rites of magic send
10   The temple prostitutes to sleep;
All the literati keep
An imaginary friend.

Cerebrotonic Cato may
Extol the ancient Disciplines,
15   But the muscle-bound Marines
Mutiny for food and pay.

Caesar's double-bed is warm
As an unimportant clerk
Writes *I DO NOT LIKE MY WORK*
20   On a pink official form.

Unendowed with wealth or pity,
Little birds with scarlet legs,
Sitting on their speckled eggs,
Eye each flu-infected city.

25   Altogether elsewhere, vast
Herds of reindeer move across
Miles and miles of golden moss,
Silently and very fast.

13 *Cerebrotonic Cato:* The medical term means "having the effect of stimulating the brain." Cato (234–149 B.C.), a consul, preached devotion to traditional Roman ideals.

The City in the Sea

Lo! Death has reared himself a throne
In a strange city lying alone
Far down within the dim West,
Where the good and the bad and the worst and the best
Have gone to their eternal rest.
There shrines and palaces and towers
(Time-eaten towers that tremble not!)
Resemble nothing that is ours.
Around, by lifting winds forgot,
Resignedly beneath the sky
The melancholy waters lie.

No rays from the holy heaven come down
On the long night-time of that town;
But light from out the lurid sea
Streams up the turrets silently —
Gleams up the pinnacles far and free —
Up domes — up spires — up kingly halls —
Up fanes — up Babylon-like walls —
Up shadowy long-forgotten bowers
Of sculptured ivy and stone flowers —
Up many and many a marvelous shrine
Whose wreathed friezes intertwine
The viol, the violet, and the vine.

Resignedly beneath the sky
The melancholy waters lie.
So blend the turrets and shadows there
That all seem pendulous in air,
While from a proud tower in the town
Death looks gigantically down.

There open fanes and gaping graves
Yawn level with the luminous waves;
But not the riches there that lie
In each idol's diamond eye —
Not the gaily-jewelled dead
Tempt the waters from their bed;

For no ripples curl, alas!
Along that wilderness of glass —
No swellings tell that winds may be
Upon some far-off happier sea —
No heaving hint that winds have been
On seas less hideously serene.

But lo, a stir is in the air!
The wave — there is a movement there!
As if the towers had thrust aside,
In slightly sinking, the dull tide —
As if their tops had feebly given
A void within the filmy Heaven.
The waves have now a redder glow —
The hours are breathing faint and low —
And when, amid no earthly moans,
Down, down that town shall settle hence,
Hell, rising from a thousand thrones,
Shall do it reverence.

40

45

50

The Day the Houses Sank

The day before the houses sank beneath the waves
There was an invasion of monarch butterflies.
Streets blazed in beating bronze.
Air shuddered like molten metal.
Trees turned to sunlight. Roofs fluttered.
Pulsing above the chimneys, they made a cloud;
Everything darkened. Warning:
North central county under a yellow alert
Until ten o'clock tonight.
But the monarchs, passing, passing
Were not stayed in their flight.

Next day the houses sank beneath the waves.
First the foundations, lapped by the oily tide;
Then lintel, windowframe, brick, eaves, tile, slate.
Now in the watery light wave after wave
Rolls overhead, crests, passes, and subsides.

Nightmare, with Angels

An angel came to me and stood by my bedside,
Remarking in a professorial-historical-economic and irritated
    voice,
"If the Romans had only invented a decent explosion-engine!
Not even the best, not even a Ford V-8

5   But, say, a Model T or even an early Napier,
They'd have built good enough roads for it (they knew how
    to build roads)
From Cape Wrath to Cape St. Vincent, Susa, Babylon and
    Moscow,
And the motorized legions never would have fallen,
And peace, in the shape of a giant eagle, would brood over
    the entire Western World!"
He changed his expression, looking now like a combination of
    Gilbert Murray, Hilaire Belloc and a dozen other scientists,

10   writers, and prophets,
And continued, in angelic tones,
"If the Greeks had known how to coöperate, if there'd never
    been a Reformation,
If Sparta had not been Sparta, and the Church had been the
    Church of the saints,
The Argive peace like a free-blooming olive-tree, the peace of
    Christ (who loved peace) like a great, beautiful vine en-
    wrapping the spinning earth!

15   Take it nearer home," he said.
"Take these Mayans and their star-clocks, their carvings and
    their great cities.
Who sacked them out of their cities, drowned the cities with
    a green jungle?
A plague? A change of climate? A queer migration?
Certainly they were skilful, certainly they created.
And, in Tenochtitlan, the dark obsidian knife and the smoking

20   heart on the stone but a fair city,
And the Incas had it worked out beautifully till Pizarro
    smashed them.
The collectivist state was there, and the ladies very agreeable.
They lacked steel, alphabet and gunpowder and they had to
    get married when the government said so.

187

They also lacked unemployment and overproduction.

25 For that matter," he said, "take the Cro-Magnons,
The fellows with the big skulls, the handsome folk, the excellent scribers of mammoths,
Physical gods and yet with the sensitive brain (they drew the fine, running reindeer).
What stopped them? What kept us all from being Apollos and Aphrodites
Only with a new taste to the nectar,
30 The laughing gods, not the cruel, the gods of song, not of war?
Supposing Aurelius, Confucius, Napoleon, Plato, Gautama, Alexander —
Just to take half a dozen —
Had ever realized and stabilized the full dream?
How long, O Lord God in the highest? How long, what now, perturbed spirit?"

He turned blue at the wingtips and disappeared as another
35 angel approached me.
This one was quietly but appropriately dressed in cellophane, synthetic rubber and stainless steel.
But his mask was the blind mask of Ares, snouted for gas-masks.
He was neither soldier, sailor, farmer, dictator nor munitions-manufacturer.
Nor did he have much conversation, except to say,
"You will not be saved by General Motors or the pre-fabricated
40 house.
You will not be saved by dialectic materialism or the Lambeth Conference.
You will not be saved by Vitamin D or the expanding universe.
In fact, you will not be saved."
Then he showed his hand:

188

In his hand was a woven, wire basket, full of seeds, small
45 metallic and shining like the seeds of portulaca;
Where he sowed them, the green vine withered, and the smoke
and the armies sprang up.

10 *Gilbert Murray:* (1866–1957), professor of Greek at Oxford, supporter of
the League of Nations; *Hilaire Belloc:* (1870–1953), British author, an
apologist for Roman Catholicism.   14 *Argive:* Greek.   20 *Tenochtitlan:*
capital of the ancient Aztecs, present site of Mexico City.   37 *Ares:*
Greek god of war (the Roman god Mars).   41 *Lambeth Conference:* meeting
of bishops of the Church of England held every ten years at Lambeth
Palace, London.

The Thumb

To end it all, the people elected a thumb.

It stood before them blankly,
as a thumb would.

Its nail flickered and blinked
in the fires people put at its feet
at night.

The people would sit with it,
holding each other, rocking.

It was strange.

What was the meaning of the cloud
joined neatly to the cuticle.
What was the cuticle doing.

Like a leader,
the thumb stood in mystery.

And what did it do? What could it do.
It pressed.

Like an iron, a tack,
like the pages of a book coming together
for the last time.

The Second Coming

Turning and turning in the widening gyre
The falcon cannot hear the falconer;
Things fall apart; the center cannot hold;
Mere anarchy is loosed upon the world,
5   The blood-dimmed tide is loosed, and everywhere
The ceremony of innocence is drowned;
The best lack all conviction, while the worst
Are full of passionate intensity.

Surely some revelation is at hand;
10   Surely the Second Coming is at hand;
The Second Coming! Hardly are those words out
When a vast image out of *Spiritus Mundi*
Troubles my sight: somewhere in sands of the desert
A shape with lion body and the head of a man,
15   A gaze blank and pitiless as the sun,
Is moving its slow thighs, while all about it
Reel shadows of the indignant desert birds.
The darkness drops again; but now I know
That twenty centuries of stony sleep
20   Were vexed to nightmare by a rocking cradle,
And what rough beast, its hour come round at last,
Slouches towards Bethlehem to be born?

Yeats, who wrote this poem in 1919, when his Ireland was in the midst of
turmoil and bloodshed, saw human history governed by the turning of
a Great Wheel whose phases influence events. Every two thousand years the
Wheel completes a turn: one civilization ends and another begins.
1 *gyre*: spiral.   12 *Spiritus Mundi*: "Soul of the World" (a term from
occultism), a collective unconscious from which each man receives
dreams, nightmares, and racial memories.

Dark Song

Sorrow how high it is
that no wall holds it
back: deep

it is that no dam undermines
it: wide that it
comes on as up a strand

multiple and relentless:
the young that are
beautiful must die; the

old, departing,
can confer
nothing.

8. Pursuing the Horizon
Journeys

I saw a man pursuing the horizon

I saw a man pursuing the horizon;
Round and round they sped.
I was disturbed at this;
I accosted the man.

"It is futile," I said,
"You can never — "

"You lie," he cried,
And ran on.

I Know a Man

As I sd to my
friend, because I am
always talking, — John, I

5   sd, which was not his
name, the darkness sur-
rounds us, what

can we do against
it, or else, shall we &
why not, buy a goddamn big car,

10   drive, he sd, for
christ's sake, look
out where yr going.

Chicken

The carhop floated up
like a white, plump, summer cloud.
Honey, I said, I've been out east
and I'm hung over.
I've been to Vermont and New Hampshire
and even to the coast of Maine.
They're crusty places, all of them,
and not easily impressed with strangers
who come blowing in from spots
like, say, Mankato or Moose Jaw.
And I've been in and out
of more damn green-shuttered windows.
Honey was patient,
just recently escaped from pig farms
and familiar with shitstorms.
She shifted a healthy cud
of some of Mr. Wrigley's finest
and pushed her boobies against the VW.
You a second-story man?
she said, trying to act sexy.
No, I said, I'm a true-story man,
honest and reliable as your daddy's watch.
Well, you talk a good game,
that's for sure, she said.
Put your best wings in a big box,
I said, suddenly very hungry.
You mean chicken? she said.
It's that kind of place, I said.
I stretched my stiff limbs
and flexed my biceps.
Hey, you're a large one, she said.
A chief is no bigger than his blanket,
I said, waving her away.

going uptown to visit miriam

on the train
old ladies playing football
going for empty seats

very funny persons

5   the train riders
                        are silly people
                        i am a train rider

but no one knows where i am
going to take this train

10   to take this train
to take this train

the ladies   read popular
paperbacks   because they
are popular   they get off
15   at 42 to change for the
westside line   or off
59 for the department store

the train pulls in & out
the white walls   dark-
20   ness   white walls   dark-
ness

ladies looking up i
wonder where they going
the dentist   pick up
25   husband pick up wife
pick up kids
pick up ?grass?
to library   to museum
to laundromat   to school

30   but no one knows where i am
going to take this train

to take this train

200

to visit miriam
to visit miriam

35 & to kiss her
on the cheek
& hope i don't
see sonia on the
street

40 but no one knows where i'm taking
this train
taking this train
to visit miriam.

Stun

If you've ever been in a car
that was hit by a train
whang
(a tearing like metal shears)
flip   spin
               "Why I'm perfectly OK!"
this streaming blood
a euphoric sweat of thanksgiving
and later
a hunk of scrap iron
just there on the turnpike
for no reason
flies up and
whang
it goes on your new underneath
well, it's like you were thrown
grabbed by the scruff of the neck
head over heels right into Proust's steamy cup
just another crumb
of scalloped cookie
odious and total memory
                             (of the cells, no doubt)
in prickle-green, speed-lashed
Massachusetts

For My Son on the Highways of His Mind

For Dan

Today the jailbird maple in the yard
sends down a thousand red hands in the rain.
Trussed at the upstairs window I
watch the great drenched leaves flap by
knowing that on the comely boulevard
incessant in your head you stand again
at the cloverleaf, thumb crooked outward.

Dreaming you travel light
guitar pick and guitar
bedroll sausage-tight
they take you as you are.

They take you as you are
there's nothing left behind
guitar pick and guitar
on the highways of your mind.

Instead you come home with two cops, your bike
lashed to the back of the cruiser because
an old lady, afraid of blacks and boys
with hair like yours, is simon-sure you took
her purse. They search you and of course you're clean.
Later we make it into a family joke,
a poor sort of catharsis. It wasn't the scene

they made — that part you rather enjoyed —
and not the old woman whose money turned up next day
in its usual lunatic place under a platter
but the principle of the thing, to be toyed
with cat and mouse, be one mouse who got away
somehow under the baseboard or radiator
and expect to be caught again sooner or later.

Dreaming you travel light
guitar pick and guitar
bedroll sausage-tight
they take you as you are.

Collar up, your discontent goes wrapped
at all times in the flannel army shirt
your father mustered out in, wars ago,
the ruptured duck still pinned to the pocket flap
and the golden toilet seat — the award his unit
won for making the bomb that killed the Japs —
now rubbed to its earliest threads, an old trousseau.

Meanwhile the posters on your bedroom wall
give up their glue. The corners start to fray.
Belmondo, Brando, Uncle Ho and Che,
last year's giants, hang lop-eared but hang on.
The merit badges, the model airplanes, all
the paraphernalia of a simpler day
gather dust on the shelf. That boy is gone.

They take you as you are
there's nothing left behind
guitar pick and guitar
on the highways of your mind.

How it will be tomorrow is anyone's guess.
The *Rand McNally* opens at a nudge
to forty-eight contiguous states, easy
as a compliant girl. In Minneapolis
I see you drinking wine under a bridge.
I see you turning on in Washington, D.C.,
panhandling in New Orleans, friendless

in Kansas City in an all-night beanery
and mugged on the beach in Venice outside L.A.
They take your watch and wallet and crack your head
as carelessly as an egg. The yolk runs red.
All this I see, or say it's what I see
in leaf fall, in rain, from the top of the stairs today
while your maps, those sweet pastels, lie flat and ready.

Dreaming you travel light
guitar pick and guitar
bedroll sausage-tight
they take you as you are.

They take you as you are
there's nothing left behind
guitar pick and guitar
on the highways of your mind.

A Friend

I walk into your house, a friend.
Your kids swarm up my steep hillsides
Or swing in my branches. Your boy rides
Me for his horsie; we pretend
Some troll threatens our lady fair.
I swing him squealing through the air
And down. Just what could I defend?

I tuck them in, sometimes, at night.
That's one secret we never tell.
Giggling in their dark room, they yell
They love me. Their father, home tonight,
Sees your girl curled up on my knee
And tells her "git" — she's bothering me.
I nod; she'd better think he's right.

Once they're in bed, he calls you "dear."
The boob-tube shows some hokum on
Adultery and loss; we yawn
Over a stale joke book and beer
Till it's your bedtime. I must leave.
I watch that squat toad pluck your sleeve.
As always, you stand shining near

Your window. I stand, Prince of Lies
Who's seen bliss; now I can drive back
Home past wreck and car lot, past shack
Slum and steelmill reddening the skies,
Past drive-ins, the hot pits where our teens
Fingerfuck and that huge screen's
Images fill their vacant eyes.

Homecoming

Even the train is taller than those shacks.
You ride past washings, smoke, and chicken-wire
And get out blushing, lugging down the tracks
Your old brown bag, and there is no one there.

5   You take a taxi, like a stranger. Your face
Swims like a fish through a dress shop, but the sky
Is always the same, and above the new blue glass
The storeys of brick are the same, paint-crusted and dry,

Unwashed when time ran through the streets. The hill
10   Has kept its cut-up mansions; and the green
Tunnel of trees you glide through is stuffed full
And choking with the shadows and the sheen

Of generations of leaves; the days of your life
Hang in the air, alive; and this is home.
15   Wherever you went you knew that they were safe.
But when the taxi meter stops and time

Stops and the bushes, snowball bushes, old
As cairns wait by the porch steps, then you know
There is no time now to recall the child
20   And ask him why he never grew up to be you.

Standing in the hall with the screen door shut
They wait for you. Think of the little town
Pressed in the star-shaped valley it has outgrown.
This sky is as low as a green-house roof.
25   And the past is dead and buried and as buried as a root.

207

Montana Pastoral

I am no shepherd of a child's surmises.
I have seen fear where the coiled serpent rises,

Thirst where the grasses burn in early May
And thistle, mustard, and the wild oat stay.

5   There is dust in this air. I saw in the heat
Grasshoppers busy in the threshing wheat.

So to this hour. Through the warm dusk I drove
To blizzards sifting on the hissing stove,

And found no images of pastoral will,
10   But fear, thirst, hunger, and this huddled chill.

Earth Walk

He drives onto the grassy shoulder and unfastens
his seat-belt. The aluminum buckle glistens.
He is watched from behind by two upholstered knobs.
He thinks: strapped to things we drive or fly,
5   helmeted for cycling and all the jobs
that peril our coconut heads, we rush
on our wheeled callings, hoping to avoid the crush,
the whooping car that blinks its bloody eye
— no Roman would be able to make sense
10   of our Latin name for it, an ambulance,
the rubber-walker with the spry attendants.

I was to go to the hospital tomorrow, but I thought
Why not today? Now I unstrap the rented Avis car
and, opening the hatch, step boldly out
15   onto the Planet Earth. My skull is bare,
thin animal hide is fitted to my feet.
The autumn air is fresh, a first pepperidge tree
has turned mahogany and red. This is a safe walk.
This turnpike is uninhabited. When I come back
20   I'll meet a trooper with a soft, wide hat
who will take away my Earth-rocks and debrief me.

Moonwalk

What sticks with me is the pit
of the walker's shadow
snatches of the white fantastic carapace
of Neil Armstrong in his

5   cautious dance and testing step
the final graceless posturing
for balance in
the moon's feeble

and uninterested hold
10   his shadow tracks behind him
he has been cautioned
and routinely vigilant looks only

sunward or at the oblique
for in the whole blackness
15   of his shadow he will be able to see
nothing   will be in effect

blind either from shadow or
the coronal glare about the black
total hole of his headshape
20   a simple diffusion effect

nothing more difficult
nothing but the illusion of sunburst
spraying outward from the crater
of the black skull   an intense

25   halo   hell I've played
that game myself before
I've had the dream where I
must be careful not to look back

the skull bursting outward and
30   the eyes brief flares like supernovae
or bombs   how
about courage then how about

210

it when the brain crumbles
clicking as it cools
35 and the teeth blackly
powder and the tongue

drains backwards down
into the belly's open pits
it is all in shadow
40 the flickering white hero

sticks with me
the walker climbs white
as salt from the grotesque ricketry
of his machine   the walker stares

45 sunward   man
is on the moon
behind him runs horizontally
the black cast of the

freezing shadow where the walker
50 must not look
back for all time the
walker must not

look
at sunrise
55 the white distance
dissolves in light before him

the sky is the memory
of no light
it is the first time
60 I have wanted to walk

here myself   I
can see the black deep
of the center drawing near
and the manshaped night remaining total

With how sad steps, O Moon, thou climb'st the skies

With how sad steps, O Moon, thou climb'st the skies!
　How silently, and with how wan a face!
　What! may it be that even in heavenly place
　That busy archer his sharp arrows tries?
Sure, if that long-with-love-acquainted eyes
　Can judge of love, thou feel'st a lover's case.
　I read it in thy looks; thy languished grace
　To me, that feel the like, thy state descries.
Then, even of fellowship, O Moon, tell me:
　Is constant love deemed there but want of wit?
　Are beauties there as proud as here they be?
Do they above love to be loved, and yet
　Those lovers scorn whom that love doth possess?
　Do they call virtue there ungratefulness?

Stars Climb Girders of Light

Stars climb girders of light.
They arrange themselves
in the usual place,
they quit before dawn,
and nothing's been done.

Then men come out.
Their helmets fill the sky;
their cities rise and fall
and the men descend,
proud carpenters of dew.

Men brief as the storm,
more than five feet of lightning,
twisted and beautiful.
Man made like his roads,
with somewhere to go.

Penny Trumpet

I had a dog like a love.
And once I had a cruel
Dream: she was a milk-pool
Around a penny trumpet.

5   I bought button-candy, bright
As bulbs on a high marquee.
My mind was like a movie
Of myself eating until —

Deep in the box — a penny
10   Trumpet like a lost light!
I stayed outside that night
In woods which were stained black,

And when the first light hauled
Itself up on its back, I heard
15   Proclaiming clock and bird
And played my penny trumpet.

And then I never stopped.
I played in every mood.
Till once, grass sang in my blood
20   While touching foot to top

With a girl who had no ear
For song and was not good
(Or so I understood).
The penny trumpet stayed

25   In my pants like a sunk boat
Trying to surface
Aright. Her face's
Remote, encircling lines

Broke in bars of light.
30   And her hard, feverish blooms —
Lips, breasts — led me to rooms
Where trumpets play all night.

9. Strong Enchantments
Magic

Her strong enchantments failing

Her strong enchantments failing,
    Her towers of fear in wreck,
Her limbecks dried of poisons
    And the knife at her neck,

The Queen of air and darkness
    Begins to shrill and cry,
'O young man, O my slayer,
    Tomorrow you shall die.'

O Queen of air and darkness,
    I think 'tis truth you say,
And I shall die tomorrow;
    But you will die today.

Thrice toss these oaken ashes in the air

Thrice toss these oaken ashes in the air,
Thrice sit thou mute in this enchanted chair;
Then thrice three times tie up this true love's knot,
And murmur soft, She will, or she will not.

5 Go burn these poisonous weeds in yon blue fire,
These screech-owl's feathers and this prickling briar,
This cypress gathered at a dead man's grave:
That all thy fears and cares an end may have.

Then come, you Fairies, dance with me a round,
10 Melt her hard heart with your melodious sound.
In vain are all the charms I can devise:
She hath an art to break them with her eyes.

Children's Runes and Omens

Hinx! minx!
The old witch winks!
The fat begins to fry.
There's nobody home
5   But Jumping Joan,
Jumping Joan and I.

*

Step on a crack,
Break your mother's back.

Step in a ditch,
10   Your mother's nose will itch.

Step in the dirt,
Tear your father's shirt.

Step on a nail,
Put your father in jail.

*

15   Dreams at night
Are the devil's delight,
Dreams in the morning
Are the angels' warning.

*

If you want to live and thrive
20   Let a spider walk alive.

*

Roll, roll, Tootsie Roll,
Roll, marble, in the hole!

(Charm used by marbles-players)

*

Can't catch me!
Can't catch me!
25   My fingers are crossed
And you can't catch me!

*

221

A scratch up and down
Is a lover found,
A scratch across
30   Is a lover lost.

                          *

If you sit on the table,
You'll be married before you're able.

                          *

Touch your collar,
Never swaller,
35   Never get the fever.

Touch your nose,
Touch your toes,
Never go in one of those!

    (Charm to be spoken when an ambulance goes by)

                          *

Drop a spoon,
40   Company soon.

Knife falls,
Gentleman calls.

Fork falls,
Lady calls.

                          *

45   Step on a beetle,
It will rain.
Pick it up and bury it,
Sun will shine again.

                          *

222

Did you eever iver over
In your leef life loaf
See the deevil divil dovil
Kiss his weef wife woaf?

No I neever niver nover
In my leef life loaf
Seed the deevil divil dovil
Kiss his weef wife woaf!

*

See a pin and pick it up,
All the day you'll have good luck.

See a pin and let it lay,
Bad luck you'll have all day.

*

Certain true,
Black and blue,
Lay me down and cut me in two.

(Lines recited to swear one is telling the truth)

*

I ring I ring a pinky!
If I tell a lie
I'll go to the bad place
Whenever I die.
White pan, black pan,
Burn me to death,
Take a big knife
And cut my breath,
Ten miles below the earth.

*

"What comes out of a chimney?"
"Smoke."

75   "May your wish and my wish never be broke."

This group of British and American nursery rimes and skip-rope jingles
has been titled by the editor. William S. and Ceil Baring-Gould explain that
the last one is "spoken when two people have said the same thing at the
same time. They should link the little fingers of their right hands while
reciting this formula" (*The Annotated Mother Goose*, New York, 1962).

The Testing-Tree

1

On my way home from school
   up tribal Providence Hill
      past the Academy ballpark
where I could never hope to play
5   I scuffed in the drainage ditch
      among the sodden seethe of leaves
hunting for perfect stones
   rolled out of glacial time
      into my pitcher's hand;
10 then sprinted lickety-
   split on my magic Keds
      from a crouching start,
scarcely touching the ground
   with my flying skin
15   as I poured it on
for the prize of mastery
   over that stretch of road,
      with no one no where to deny
when I flung myself down
20   that on the given course
      I was the world's fastest human.

2

Around the bend
   that tried to loop me home
      dawdling came natural
25 across a nettled field
   riddled with rabbit-life
      where the bees sank sugar-wells
in the trunks of the maples
   and a stringy old lilac
30   more than two stories tall
blazing with mildew
   remembered a door in the

                    long teeth of the woods.
            All of it happened slow:
35   brushing the stickseed off,
                            wading through jewelweed
            strangled by angel's hair,
                    spotting the print of the deer
                            and the red fox's scats.

40   Once I owned the key
                    to an umbrageous trail
                            thickened with mosses
            where flickering presences
                    gave me right of passage
45   as I followed in the steps
            of straight-backed Massassoit
                    soundlessly heel-and-toe
                            practicing my Indian walk.

            3

            Past the abandoned quarry
50   where the pale sun bobbed
                            in the sump of the granite,
            past copperhead ledge,
                    where the ferns gave foothold,
                            I walked, deliberate,
55   on to the clearing,
                    with the stones in my pocket
                            changing to oracles
            and my coiled ear tuned
                    to the slightest leaf-stir.
60   I had kept my appointment.
            There I stood in the shadow,
                    at fifty measured paces,
                            of the inexhaustible oak,
            tyrant and target,
65   Jehovah of acorns,

              watchtower of the thunders,
       that locked King Philip's War
            in its annulated core
                under the cut of my name.
70   *Father wherever you are*
            I have only three throws
                bless my good right arm.
   In the haze of afternoon,
            while the air flowed saffron,
75   I played my game for keeps —
   for love, for poetry,
            and for eternal life —
                after the trials of summer.

   4

   In the recurring dream
80   my mother stands
               in her bridal gown
   under the burning lilac,
            with Bernard Shaw and Bertie
               Russell kissing her hands;
85   the house behind her is in ruins;
            she is wearing an owl's face
               and makes barking noises.
   Her minatory finger points.
            I pass through the cardboard doorway
90   askew in the field
   and peer down a well
            where an albino walrus huffs.
              He has the gentlest eyes.
   If the dirt keeps sifting in,
95   staining the water yellow,
              why should I be blamed?
   Never try to explain.
            That single Model A
              sputtering up the grade

227

unfurled a highway behind
    where the tanks maneuver,
      revolving their turrets.
In a murderous time
    the heart breaks and breaks
      and lives by breaking.
It is necessary to go
    through dark and deeper dark
      and not to turn.
I am looking for the trail.
    Where is my testing-tree?
      Give me back my stones!

In his note to this poem Stanley Kunitz wrote: "When I was a boy in Worcester, Massachusetts, my family lived on top of a hill, at the thin edge of the city, with the woods beyond. Much of the time I was alone, but I learned how not to be lonely, exploring the surrounding fields and the old Indian trails. In the games that I improvised, most of them involved with running, climbing, and a variety of ball-skills, I was a fierce competitor, representing in turn myself and my imaginary opponent. It did not occur to me to be surprised that 'I' was always the winner.

"The stone-throwing that figures in the poem was of a somewhat special order, since it did more than try my skill: it challenged destiny. My life hinged on the three throws permitted me, according to my rules. If I hit the target-oak once, somebody would love me; if I hit it twice, I should be a poet; if I scored all three times, I should never die. A friend of mine tells me that what I have recorded here is recognizable as an ancient ritual, and that the patriarchal scarred oak, as I have described it, is transparently a manifestation of the King of the Wood. Such mysteries for a Worcester childhood!"

Charming the Moon

At the ford, while grass-green frogs
continue and continue their high singing,

we crush wild fennel in our hands, a charm
to keep the magic going strong. Well,

5   we are animals, we say, and our children
are animals, and we will all survive.

The water in the creek runs silver, quick,
upstream to the moon, and down the canyon

to the sea, through rocks, moss, past frogs.
10   Everywhere the evidence of continuing:

under the pavement sow-bugs, white grubs,
slick tendrils drill; through trees,

sycamore, live oak, the quarter moon
is rising, falling, appearing, disappearing,

15   around each curve of Mountain Drive.
An opossum, round shadow, wavers in shadow.

We will survive. The moon will draw back
softly at the touch of the astronaut's foot,

and with wild fennel we'll charm it right
20   again, for all us animals, and green frogs

at the ford. Here's the real moon, in cupped
hands in the water. Drink, children, sing.

A Magus

A missionary from the Mau Mau told me.
   There are spores blowing from space.
   He has himself seen an amazing botany
   springing the crust. Fruit with a bearded face
   that howls at the picker. Mushrooms that bleed.
   A tree of enormous roots that sends no trace
   above ground; not a leaf. And he showed me the seed
   of thorned lettuces that induce
   languages. The Jungle has come loose,
   is changing purpose.
                 Nor are the vegetations
of the new continuum the only sign.
New eyes have observed the constellations.
And what does not change when looked at? — coastline?
sea? sky? The propaganda of the wind reaches.
Set watches on your gardens. What spring teaches
seed shall make new verbs. A root is a tongue.

I repeat it as he spoke it. I do not interpret
   what I do not understand. He comes among
   many who have come to us. He speaks and we forget
   and are slow to be reminded. But he does come,
   signs do appear.
               There are poisoned islands far over:
   fish from their reefs come to table and some
   glow in the dark not of candlelight. A windhover
   chatters in the counters of our polar camps.
   A lectern burns. Geese jam the radar. The red phone
   rings. Is there an answer? Planes from black ramps
   howl to the edge of sound. The unknown
   air breaks from them. They crash through.
   What time is it in orbit? Israeli teams
   report they have found the body, but Easter seems
   symbolically secure. Is a fact true?

How many megatons of idea is a man? What island
  lies beyond his saying? I have heard, and say
  what I heard said and believe. I do not understand.
  But I have seen him change water to blood, and call away
  the Lion from its Empire. He speaks that tongue.
  I have seen white bird and black bird follow him, hung
  like one cloud over his head. His hand,
  when he wills it, bursts into flame. The white bird
  and the black divide and circle it. At his word
  they enter the fire and glow like metal. A ray
  reaches from him to the top of the air,
  and in it the figures of a vision play
  these things I believe whose meaning I cannot say.

Then he closes his fist and there is nothing there.

Witch Doctor

I

He dines alone surrounded by reflections
of himself. Then after sleep and benzedrine
descends the Cinquecento stair his magic
wrought from hypochondria of the well-
to-do and nagging deathwish of the poor;
swirls on smiling genuflections of
his liveried chauffeur into a crested
lilac limousine, the cynosure
of mousey neighbors tittering behind
Venetian blinds and half afraid of him
and half admiring his outrageous flair.

II.

Meanwhile his mother, priestess in gold lamé,
precedes him to the quondam theater
now Israel Temple of the Highest Alpha,
where the bored, the sick, the alien, the tired
await euphoria. With deadly vigor
she prepares the way for mystery
and lucre. Shouts in blues-contralto, "He's
God's dictaphone of all-redeeming truth.
Oh he's the holyweight champeen who's come
to give the knockout lick to your bad luck;
say he's the holyweight champeen who's here
to deal a knockout punch to your hard luck."

III.

Reposing on cushions of black leopard skin,
he telephones instructions for a long
slow drive across the park that burgeons now
with spring and sailors. Peers questingly
into the green fountainous twilight, sighs
and turns the gold-plate dial to Music For

30 Your Dining-Dancing Pleasure. Smoking Egyptian
cigarettes rehearses in his mind
a new device that he must use tonight.

IV.

Approaching Israel Temple, mask in place,
he hears ragtime allegros of a "Song
35 of Zion" that becomes when he appears
a hallelujah wave for him to walk.
His mother and a rainbow-surpliced cordon
conduct him choiring to the altar-stage,
and there he kneels and seems to pray before
40 a lighted Jesus painted sealskin-brown.
Then with a glittering flourish he arises,
turns, gracefully extends his draperied arms:
"Israelites, true Jews, O found lost tribe
of Israel, receive my blessing now.
45 Selah, selah." He feels them yearn toward him
as toward a lover, exults before the image
of himself their trust gives back. Stands as though
in meditation, letting their eyes caress
his garments jewelled and chatoyant, cut
50 to fall, to flow from his tall figure
dramatically just so.Then all at once
he sways, quivers, gesticulates as if
to ward off blows or kisses, and when he speaks
again he utters wildering vocables,
55 hypnotic no-words planned (and never failing)
to enmesh his flock in theopathic tension.
Cries of eudaemonic pain attest
his artistry. Behind the mask he smiles.
And now in subtly altering light he chants
60 and sinuously trembles, chants and trembles
while convulsive energies of eager faith
surcharge the theater with power of

233

their own, a power he has counted on
and for a space allows to carry him.
65 Dishevelled antiphons proclaim the moment
his followers all day have hungered for,
but which is his alone.
He signals: tambourines begin, frenetic
drumbeat and glissando. He dances from the altar,
70 robes hissing, flaring, shimmering; down aisles
where mantled guardsmen intercept wild hands
that arduously strain to clutch his vestments,
he dances, dances, ensorcelled and aloof,
the fervid juba of God as lover, healer,
75 conjurer. And of himself as God.

The Great Silkie of Sule Skerry

An eartly nourris sits and sings,
    And aye she sings, "Ba, lily wean!
Little ken I my bairnis father,
    Far less the land that he staps in."

5 Then ane arose at her bed-fit,
    An' a grumly guest I'm sure was he:
"Here am I, thy bairnis father,
    Although that I be not comelie.

"I am a man upo the lan,
10   An' I am a silkie in the sea,
And when I'm far and far frae lan,
    My dwelling is in Sule Skerrie."

"It was na weel," quo the maiden fair,
    "It was na weel, indeed," quo she,
15 "That the Great Silkie of Sule Skerrie
    Suld hae come and aught a bairn to me."

Now he has taen a purse of goud,
    And he has pat it upo her knee,
Sayin, "Gie to me my little young son,
20   An' tak thee up thy nourris-fee.

"An' it sall come to pass on a simmer's day,
    When the sin shines het on evera stane,
That I will tak my little young son,
    An' teach him for to swim the faem.

25 "An' thu sall marry a proud gunner,
    An' a proud gunner I'm sure he'll be,
An' the very first shot that ere he shoots,
    He'll shoot baith my young son and me."

Sule Skerry is an island in the Orkney group, north of Scotland, where
there abound many stories of the silkies, or seal-people. As revealed in this
traditional popular ballad, a silkie can venture upon land, change his
shape, and live among men.   1 *nourris:* nurse, mother.   2 *Ba, lily wean!:*
lullaby words.   4 *staps:* dwells.   5 *ane:* one.   *bed-fit:* foot of her bed.
6 *grumly:* fearsome.   16 *aught:* fathered.

The Demon Lover

"O where have you been, my long, long love,
    This long seven years and mair?"
"O I'm come to seek my former vows
    Ye granted me before."

"O hold your tongue of your former vows,
    For they will breed sad strife;
O hold your tongue of your former vows,
    For I am become a wife."

He turned him right and round about,
    And the tear blinded his ee:
"I wad never hae trodden on Irish ground
    If it had not been for thee.

"I might hae had a king's daughter,
    Far, far beyond the sea.
I might have had a king's daughter
    Had it not been for love o thee."

"If ye might have had a king's daughter,
    Yer sel ye had to blame.
Ye might have taken the king's daughter,
    For ye kend that I was nane.

"If I was to leave my husband dear,
    And my two babes also,
O what have you to take me to
    If with you I should go?"

"I hae seven ships upon the sea —
    The eighth brought me to land —
With four-and-twenty bold mariners,
    And music on every hand."

She has taken up her two little babes,
    Kissed them baith cheek and chin:
"O fair ye weel, my ain two babes,
    For I'll never see you again."

She set her foot upon the ship;
  No mariners could she behold,
35 But the sails were o the taffetie
  And the masts o the beaten gold.

They had not sailed a league, a league,
  A league but barely three,
When dismal grew his countenance,
40 And drumlie grew his ee.

They had not sailed a league, a league,
  A league but barely three,
Until she espied his cloven foot,
  And she wept right bitterlie.

45 "O hold your tongue of your weeping," says he,
  "Of your weeping now let me be.
I will shew you how the lilies grow
  On the banks of Italy."

"O what hills are yon, yon pleasant hills
50 That the sun shines sweetly on?"
"O yon are the hills of Heaven," he said,
  "Where you will never win."

"O whaten mountain is yon," she said,
  "All so dreary wi frost and snow?"
55 "O yon is the mountain of Hell," he cried,
  "Where you and I will go."

He strack the tap-mast wi his hand,
    The fore-mast wi his knee,
And he brake that gallant ship in twain,
60   And sank her in the sea.

This version of "The Demon Lover" (also known as "James Harris" and, in America, "The House Carpenter") comes from Sir Walter Scott's collection of popular ballads, *Minstrelsy of the Scottish Border*. According to a broadside version of the late seventeenth century, Jane Reynolds and James Harris had been betrothed, but the young man was impressed as a sailor. Believing him dead, Jane married a carpenter. Several versions are collected by F. J. Child in *The English and Scottish Popular Ballads* (number 243).   40 *drumlie:* dreary.

The Two Sisters

1.

Was two sisters loved one man,
   Jelly flower jan;
   The rose marie;
   The jury hangs o'er
   The rose marie.

2.

He loved the youngest a little the best,
   Jelly flower jan;
   The rose marie;
   The jury hangs o'er
   The rose marie.

3.

Them two sisters going down stream,
   Jelly flower jan;
   The rose marie;
   The jury hangs o'er
   The rose marie.

4.

The oldest pushed the youngest in,
   Jelly flower jan;
   The rose marie;
   The jury hangs o'er
   The rose marie.

5.

She made a fiddle out of her bones,
   Jelly flower jan;
   The rose marie;
   The jury hangs o'er
25   The rose marie.

6.

She made the screws out of her fingers,
   Jelly flower jan;
   The rose marie;
   The jury hangs o'er
30   The rose marie.

7.

She made the strings out of her hair,
   Jelly flower jan;
   The rose marie;
   The jury hangs o'er
35   The rose marie.

8.

The first string says, "Yonder sets my sister on a rock
   Tying of a true-love's knot,"
   Jelly flower jan;
   The rose marie;
   The jury hangs o'er
40   The rose marie.

9.

The next string says, "She pushed me in the deep so far."
   Jelly flower jan;
   The rose marie;
   The jury hangs o'er
45   The rose marie.

This Anglo-American folk song, a variant of a traditional ballad (number 10 in F. J. Child's *The English and Scottish Popular Ballads*), was collected in this version by Mrs. Mellinger Henry from Mrs. Samuel Harmon of Cade's Cove, Blount County, Tennessee, in 1930.

The House o' the Mirror

Upon the hill my lover stands.
A burning branch is in his hands.
He stamps impatient on the stane,
And calls, and claims me for his ain.

5   I bolt my door. I hood my light.
I rin tae slam the shutters tight.
I tug my curtains claise and thick.
I stop my clock lest it should tick.

My house is dark. My house is still.
10   He shines and thunders on the hill.
I pace the rooms, and as I pass
My een glint sidelang towards the glass.

The glass is tall and like a gate.
My image watches while I wait
15   For him tae loup the hill o' night
And raze my house wi' heavenly light.

At his approach I'm like tae dee
Sae hard my hert belabors me.
My house o' stane is frail as straw
20   For at a clap its wa's doun fa'.

But wae's my hert, for weel I ken
He craves a love ne'er found by men,
Hungering for yon eldrich lass
Wha haunts the darkness o' the glass.

25   The ghaist that in the mirror gleams,
Floating aloof, like one wha dreams.
For her he rages, mad and blind,
And plunders a' my flesh tae find.

He dives within my body's deeps
30   Tae fathom whaur the phantom sleeps.
He shrieks because he canna clutch
What lies beyond the grief o' touch.

Aye, though we strauchle breast tae breast,
And kiss sae hard we cry for rest,
And daur a' pleasures till they cloy,
We find nae peace and little joy.

For still between us moves the shade
That ne'er will lie beneath his plaid.
A' but my ghaist tae him I give.
My ghaist nae man may touch and live.

Oh! mirror like the midnight sky,
Sae high and dark, sae dark and high,
There bides my wraith remote frae men
In warlds nae earthly lovers ken.

My flesh is starvit morn and night
For a' love's horror and delight.
My ghaist apart frae passion stands.
It is my ghaist that love demands.

While blood dunts loud agin mine ear,
And banes grow weak wi' blissful fear,
Upon the hill my lover manes
For what has neither blood nor banes.

35

40

45

50

15 *loup:* leap.   33 *strauchle:* struggle.   35 *daur:* work.   45 *dunts:* thumps.

243

Ballad of No Proper Man

As I was going down the lane
And my love's hand holding my hand
I met a man, no proper man
With a turn and a caper on the sand.

'She will come with me,' he said,
'I'll take your love's hand in my hand.
You can wither in a narrow bed
And I will caper on the sand.'

'I will not let my love leave me,
I'll hold her hand close in my hand
Until the tide empties the sea
For all your capers on the sand;

'My love stays here by my right side,
Her hand holds fast within my hand
Till the last sprig on the yew has died
Though you tumble on the sand,'

I cried defiance in his teeth
Who clasped my love's hand in his hand.
Cold was the wind that clenched my breath
And skittered across the gritty sand.

Yesterday the waves lunged high
When my love's hand held to my hand.
The hollow deeps are stony dry.
Who is that capers on the sand?

Last night the green fields sucked the dew
When my hand cleaved to my love's hand.
The wind now rattles a withered bough
And turns and capers on the sand.

My love my love where are you gone
Who held my hand tight in your hand?
My heart shakes bars of narrow rib-bone.
Who is that capers on the sand?

For the El Paso Weather Bureau

In the heat of the day a funnel cloud
was sighted north of the Franklin Mountains.
out on their lawns seeing it move the residents
took off their guns, went to their knees;
5   touched fingertips to lips. closer
they saw how something like a sheik
sat in its middle playing a flute.
sparks shot from his head
and around him butterflies
10   on gold chains floated through the spirals.
they smelled flesh burning. in the gloom
some had roses spread like wounds over foreheads
and chests, that dripped
a viscid liquid, clear sperm
15   on the ground. they prayed harder.
it never touched down.

Kubla Khan

or A Vision in a Dream. A Fragment

In Xanadu did Kubla Khan
A stately pleasure dome decree:
Where Alph, the sacred river, ran
Through caverns measureless to man
5 Down to a sunless sea.
So twice five miles of fertile ground
With walls and towers were girdled round:
And there were gardens bright with sinuous rills,
Where blossomed many an incense-bearing tree;
10 And here were forests ancient as the hills,
Enfolding sunny spots of greenery.

But oh! that deep romantic chasm which slanted
Down the green hill athwart a cedarn cover!
A savage place! as holy and enchanted
15 As e'er beneath a waning moon was haunted
By woman wailing for her demon lover!
And from this chasm, with ceaseless turmoil seething,
As if this earth in fast thick pants were breathing,
A mighty fountain momently was forced:
20 Amid whose swift half-intermitted burst
Huge fragments vaulted like rebounding hail,
Or chaffy grain beneath the thresher's flail:
And 'mid these dancing rocks at once and ever
It flung up momently the sacred river.
25 Five miles meandering with a mazy motion
Through wood and dale the sacred river ran,
Then reached the caverns measureless to man,
And sank in tumult to a lifeless ocean:
And 'mid this tumult Kubla heard from far
30 Ancestral voices prophesying war!
  The shadow of the dome of pleasure
  Floated midway on the waves;
  Where was heard the mingled measure
  From the fountain and the caves.
35 It was a miracle of rare device,

A sunny pleasure-dome with caves of ice!
   A damsel with a dulcimer
   In a vision once I saw:
   It was an Abyssinian maid,
40   And on her dulcimer she played,
   Singing of Mount Abora.
   Could I revive within me
   Her symphony and song,
   To such a deep delight 'twould win me,
45 That with music loud and long,
I would build that dome in air,
That sunny dome! those caves of ice!
And all who heard should see them there,
And all should cry, Beware! Beware!
50 His flashing eyes, his floating hair!
Weave a circle round him thrice,
And close your eyes with holy dread,
For he on honey-dew hath fed,
And drunk the milk of Paradise.

There was an actual Kublai Khan, a thirteenth-century Mongol emperor,
and a Chinese city of Xamdu, but Coleridge's dream vision also borrows from
travelers' descriptions of other exotic places such as Abyssinia and America.
51 *circle:* a magic circle drawn to keep away evil spirits.

The Dream

O God, in the dream the terrible horse began
To paw at the air, and make for me with his blows.
Fear kept for thirty-five years poured through his mane,
And retribution equally old, or nearly, breathed through
     his nose.

5   Coward complete, I lay and wept on the ground
When some strong creature appeared, and leapt for the rein.
Another woman, as I lay half in a swound,
Leapt in the air, and clutched at the leather and chain.

Give him, she said, something of yours as a charm.
10 Throw him, she said, some poor thing you alone claim.
No, no, I cried, he hates me; he's out for harm,
And whether I yield or not, it is all the same.

But, like a lion in a legend, when I flung the glove
Pulled from my sweating, my cold right hand,
15 The terrible beast, that no one may understand,
Came to my side, and put down his head in love.

The Song of Wandering Aengus

I went out to the hazel wood,
Because a fire was in my head,
And cut and peeled a hazel wand,
And hooked a berry to a thread;
And when white moths were on the wing,
And moth-like stars were flickering out,
I dropped the berry in a stream
And caught a little silver trout.

When I had laid it on the floor
I went to blow the fire aflame,
But something rustled on the floor,
And some one called me by my name:
It had become a glimmering girl
With apple blossom in her hair
Who called me by my name and ran
And faded through the brightening air.

Though I am old with wandering
Through hollow lands and hilly lands,
I will find out where she has gone,
And kiss her lips and take her hands;
And walk among long dappled grass,
And pluck till time and times are done
The silver apples of the moon,
The golden apples of the sun.

Consumed ✓

Why should you believe in magic,
pretend an interest in astrology
or the tarot? Truth is, you are

free, and what might happen to you
today, nobody knows. And your
personality may undergo a radical

transformation in the next half
hour. So it goes. You are consumed
by your faith in justice, your

hope for a better day, the rightness
of fate, the dreams, the lies
the taunts. — Nobody gets what he

wants. A dark star passes through
you on your way home from
the grocery: never again are you

the same — an experience which is
impossible to forget, impossible
to share. The longing to be pure

is over. You are the stranger
who gets stranger by the hour.

10. Looking Down for Miles
Solitude

Mid-August at
Sourdough Mountain Lookout

Down valley a smoke haze
Three days heat, after five days rain
Pitch glows on the fir-cones
Across rocks and meadows
Swarms of new flies.

I cannot remember things I once read
A few friends, but they are in cities.
Drinking cold snow-water from a tin cup
Looking down for miles
Through high still air.

Anticipation of Sharks

stay silent
keep away from sharks. stay
away from blood,
you will not be able to deal with a missing leg,
in the water / you will bleed to death,
you will be the pain of a yard strewn with brown leaves,
and the shark will rake you clean,
strip your bones to their earth.

stay silent,
when you are in danger. The night is deep water.
The dark is a path of sharks,
their teeth flash
as the constellations.

The lonely night passes over me
as a submarine.
I am always lonely, will be
until I find someone to share my life with.
How lucky you are, good friend, to have taken up trout fishing.
I swim with sharks. They mistake me
for relatives.
We have nothing cold in common
but we glitter at each other.

And I stay silent,
as I swim in these waters,
more alone
than if I were by myself.

Zimmer Drunk and Alone, Dreaming of Old Football Games

I threw the inside of my gizzard out, splashing
Down the steps of that dark football stadium
Where I had gone to celebrate the ancient games.
But I had been gut-blocked and cut down by
A two-ton guard in one quarter of my fifth.
Fireflies broke and smeared upon my eyes,
And the half-moon spiraled on my corneas.
Between spasms the crickets beat halftime to
My tympanum, and stars twirled like fire batons
Inside the darkness. The small roll at my gut's end,
Rising like a cheer, curled up intestine to the stomach,
Quaking to my gullet, and out my tongue again.
Out came old victories, defeats and scoreless ties,
Out came all the quarters of my fifth,
Until exhausted, my wind gone and my teeth sour,
I climbed the high fence out of that dark stadium,
Still smarting from the booing and hard scrimmage.
I zigzagged down the street, stiff-arming buildings,
And giving flashy hip fakes to the lamp posts.
I cut for home, a veteran broken field drunkard,
With my bottle tucked up high away from fumbles.

Mr. Flood's Party

Old Eben Flood, climbing alone one night
Over the hill between the town below
And the forsaken upland hermitage
That held as much as he should ever know
On earth again of home, paused warily.
The road was his with not a native near;
And Eben, having leisure, said aloud,
For no man else in Tilbury Town to hear:

"Well, Mr. Flood, we have the harvest moon
Again, and we may not have many more;
The bird is on the wing, the poet says,
And you and I have said it here before.
Drink to the bird." He raised up to the light
The jug that he had gone so far to fill,
And answered huskily: "Well, Mr. Flood,
Since you propose it, I believe I will."

Alone, as if enduring to the end
A valiant armor of scarred hopes outworn,
He stood there in the middle of the road
Like Roland's ghost winding a silent horn.
Below him, in the town among the trees,
Where friends of other days had honored him,
A phantom salutation of the dead
Rang thinly till old Eben's eyes were dim.

Then, as a mother lays her sleeping child
Down tenderly, fearing it may awake,
He set the jug down slowly at his feet
With trembling care, knowing that most things break;
And only when assured that on firm earth
It stood, as the uncertain lives of men
Assuredly did not, he paced away,
And with his hand extended paused again:

"Well, Mr. Flood, we have not met like this
In a long time; and many a change has come

35 To both of us, I fear, since last it was
    We had a drop together. Welcome home!"
    Convivially returning with himself,
    Again he raised the jug up to the light;
    And with an acquiescent quaver said:
40 "Well, Mr. Flood, if you insist, I might.

    "Only a very little, Mr. Flood —
    For auld lang syne. No more, sir; that will do."
    So, for the time, apparently it did,
    And Eben evidently thought so too;
45 For soon amid the silver loneliness
    Of night he lifted up his voice and sang,
    Secure, with only two moons listening,
    Until the whole harmonious landscape rang —

    "For auld lang syne." The weary throat gave out;
50 The last word wavered, and the song was done.
    He raised again the jug regretfully
    And shook his head, and was again alone.
    There was not much that was ahead of him,
    And there was nothing in the town below —
55 Where strangers would have shut the many doors
    That many friends had opened long ago.

11 *the poet:* Omar Khayyám, Persian poet, a praiser of wine, whose
Rubáiyát, translated by Edward FitzGerald, included these lines:
>   Come, fill the Cup, and in the fire of Spring
>   Your Winter-garment of Repentance fling:
>   The Bird of Time has but a little way
>   To flutter and the Bird is on the wing.

20 *Roland's ghost . . . horn:* In the battle of Roncesvalles, the medieval
French hero Roland fought to his death, refusing to sound his horn for help
until all hope was gone.

The Ballad of Mary Baldwin

On Third Street there's a naked spot
where a dead dog rotted the green grass plot.
What wouldn't they do if they found out who the person was
    who did it?
Ginny asked if there was a way
and Johnny too, to make it O.K.
Mother's not sure — not sure she's cross;
I still come running, and she's still boss
except what I do when she wants to know who the person was
    who did it.

     The grass is green, the roses are red.
     Do up the dishes and go to bed.

My father looked like he didn't hear,
but after he heard he shed a tear;
he swore what he'd do if I'd tell him who the man it was
    who did it.
I sat at my window and watched the trees.
I cried and said, "Do what you please."
Father and mother took the car,
they went to the city and went to a bar.
What else could they do? They didn't know who the man it
    was who did it.

     O the grass is green, and roses are red.
     Do up the dishes and go to bed.

I heard of a nurse in another town
who made no fuss and made no frown
and did it for you, if you forgot who the person was who fixed it.
I sat in the house for a week or so,
I didn't have the mind to go
until I thought it couldn't wait.
But she said, for her it was too late.
What should I do, and I so new and never before had done it?

>The grass is green, the roses are red.
30   >Dishes are dishes, and go to bed.

She said, some women four times a year
scrape out the motherhood they fear,
that's what they do, and they don't care who the people are
    who did it.
I found a doctor who said he could,
35   he shouldn't, but — for a price he would.
Next week the doctor went to his farm,
he slipped on a rock and broke his arm.
There was nothing to do when the one man who could do it
    couldn't do it.

>The grass grows tall, the roses red.
40   >Do up the dishes and go to bed.

Mother and father, Ginny and John
stopped talking, but their eyes kept on
saying what can you do when she won't tell who the boy it was
    who did it.
Walk to the corner. Walk by the lake.
45   People, people make me shake.
On Third Street I saw a naked spot
where a dead dog rots the green grass plot.
What good would it do if I did tell who the young man was
    who did it?

>The grass grows green, and roses red.
50   >Go do the dishes. Go to bed.

Lonesome in the Country

How much of me is sandwiches radio beer?
How much pizza traffic & neon messages?
I take thoughtful journeys to supermarkets,
philosophize about the newest good movie,
camp out at magazine racks & on floors,
catch humanity leering back in laundromats,
invent shortcuts by the quarter hour

There's meaning to all this itemization
& I'd do well to look for it in woodpiles
or in hills & springs or trees in the woods
instead of staying in the shack all the time
imagining too much
                           falling asleep in old chairs

All that childhood I spent in farmhouses
& still cant tell one bush from another —
Straight wilderness would wipe me out
faster than cancer from cigarette smoke

Meantime my friends are out all day long
stomping thru the woods all big-eyed
& that's me walking the road afternoons
head in a book
                           all that hilly sweetness wasting

A Walk in March

Somewhere near here a new-loosed creek sloughs down
to the Merrimack through dead cattails. Night slides
about the skin, blood-heat, outside,
until, years lapsed, I itch to scratch it off
and let the blackness gorging its skin balloon

blow free, be simple component of the night.
The air stinks of borning things; reborn things
roll back their stones. Spring — never easier
of access. Sixteen, we clotted at drugstore
corners evenings, watching the one some called

whore swaying her boneless body past
the hardware store, each pore and fold and chink
of flesh and fabric redolent of sin; her ass,
brassily censer-swinging, trailed a secretion
of electric musk through the elmed street.

She bore her mystery as the priest his
and we knelt openmouthed at her altar rail,
sick with ignorance. Never too old:
black calls to black yet through the straining skin.
It is the darkest night of the year, and starless.

Ribald romeos less and less berattle

Ribald romeos less and less berattle
your shut window with impulsive pebbles.
Sleep — who cares? — the clock around. The door hugs
        firmly in its framework,
5   which once, oh how promptly it popped open
easy hinges. And so rarely heard now
"Night after night I'm dying for you, darling!
        You — you just lie there."
Tit for tat. For insolent old lechers
10   you will weep soon on the lonely curbing
while, above, the dark of the moon excites the
        wind from the mountain.
Then, deep down, searing desire (libido
that deranges, too, old rutting horses)
15   in your riddled abdomen is raging
        not without heartache
that the young boys take their solace rather
in the greener ivy, the green myrtle;
and such old winter-bitten sticks and stems they
20   figure the hell with.

This is a translation from the Latin poet Horace (*Odes* I, 25).

Resolution and Independence

There was a roaring in the wind all night;
The rain came heavily and fell in floods;
But now the sun is rising calm and bright;
The birds are singing in the distant woods;
Over his own sweet voice the stock-dove broods;
The jay makes answer as the magpie chatters;
And all the air is filled with pleasant noise of waters.

All things that love the sun are out of doors;
The sky rejoices in the morning's birth;
The grass is bright with rain-drops; — on the moors
The hare is running races in her mirth;
And with her feet she from the plashy earth
Raises a mist; that, glittering in the sun,
Runs with her all the way, wherever she doth run.

I was a traveler then upon the moor;
I saw the hare that raced about with joy;
I heard the woods and distant waters roar;
Or heard them not, as happy as a boy:
The pleasant season did my heart employ:
My old remembrances went from me wholly:
And all the ways of men, so vain and melancholy.

But, as it sometimes chanceth, from the might
Of joy in minds that can no further go,
As high as we have mounted in delight
In our dejection do we sink as low;
To me that morning did it happen so;
And fears and fancies thick upon me came;
Dim sadness — and blind thoughts, I knew not, nor could name.

I heard the skylark warbling in the sky;
And I bethought me of the playful hare:
Even such a happy child of earth am I;
Even as these blissful creatures do I fare;
Far from the world I walk, and from all care;
But there may come another day to me —
Solitude, pain of heart, distress, and poverty.

My whole life I have lived in pleasant thought,
As if life's business were a summer mood;
As if all needful things would come unsought
To genial faith, still rich in genial good;
40 But how can He expect that others should
Build for him, sow for him, and at his call
Love him, who for himself will take no heed at all?

I thought of Chatterton, the marvelous Boy,
The sleepless soul that perished in his pride;
45 Of him who walked in glory and in joy
Following his plough, along the mountainside:
By our own spirits are we deified:
We poets in our youth begin in gladness:
But thereof come in the end despondency and madness.

50 Now, whether it were by peculiar grace,
A leading from above, a something given,
Yet it befell that, in this lonely place,
When I with these untoward thoughts had striven,
Beside a pool bare to the eye of heaven
55 I saw a Man before me unawares:
The oldest man he seemed that ever wore grey hairs.

As a huge stone is sometimes seen to lie
Couched on the bald top of an eminence;
Wonder to all who do the same espy,
60 By what means it could thither come, and whence;
So that it seems a thing endued with sense:
Like a sea-beast crawled forth, that on a shelf
Of rock or sand reposeth, there to sun itself;

Such seemed this Man, not all alive nor dead,
65 Nor all asleep — in his extreme old age:
His body was bent double, feet and head
Coming together in life's pilgrimage;
As if some dire constraint of pain, or rage
Of sickness felt by him in times long past,
70 A more than human weight upon his frame had cast.

266

Himself he propped, limbs, body, and pale face,
Upon a long grey staff of shaven wood:
And, still as I drew near with gentle pace,
Upon the margin of that moorish flood
75   Motionless as a cloud the old Man stood,
That heareth not the loud winds when they call;
And moveth all together, if it move at all.

At length, himself unsettling, he the pond
Stirred with his staff, and fixedly did look
80   Upon the muddy water, which he conned,
As if he had been reading in a book:
And now a stranger's privilege I took;
And, drawing to his side, to him did say,
"This morning gives us promise of a glorious day."

85   A gentle answer did the old Man make,
In courteous speech which forth he slowly drew:
And him with further words I thus bespake,
"What occupation do you there pursue?
This is a lonesome place for one like you."
90   Ere he replied, as flash of mild surprise
Broke from the sable orbs of his yet-vivid eyes.

His words came feebly, from a feeble chest,
But each in solemn order followed each,
With something of a lofty utterance drest —
95   Choice word and measured phrase, above the reach
Of ordinary men; a stately speech;
Such as grave Livers do in Scotland use,
Religious men, who give to God and man their dues.

He told, that to these waters he had come
100   To gather leeches, being old and poor:
Employment hazardous and wearisome!
And he had many hardships to endure:
From pond to pond he roamed, from moor to moor;
Housing, with God's help, by choice or chance;
105   And in this way he gained an honest maintenance.

The old Man still stood talking by my side;
But now *his* voice to me was like a stream
Scarce heard; nor word from word could I divide;
And the whole body of the Man did seem
110 Like one whom I had met with in a dream;
Or like a man from some far region sent,
To give me human strength, by apt admonishment.

My former thoughts returned: the fear that kills;
And hope that is unwilling to be fed;
115 Cold, pain, and labor, and all fleshy ills;
And mighty poets in their misery dead.
— Perplexed, and longing to be comforted
My question eagerly did I renew,
"How is it that you live, and what is it you do?"

120 He with a smile did then his words repeat;
And said that, gathering leeches, far and wide
He traveled; stirring thus about his feet
The waters of the pools where they abide.
"Once I could meet with them on every side;
125 But they have dwindled long by slow decay;
Yet still I persevere, and find them where I may."

While he was talking thus, the lonely place,
The old Man's shape, and speech — all troubled me:
In my mind's eye I seemed to see him pace
130 About the weary moors continually,
Wandering about alone and silently.
While I these thoughts within myself pursued,
He, having made a pause, the same discourse renewed.

And soon with this he other matter blended,
135   Cheerfully uttered, with demeanor kind,
But stately in the main; and, when he ended,
I could have laughed myself to scorn to find
In that decrepit Man so firm a mind.
"God," said I, "be my help and stay secure;
140   I'll think of the Leech-gatherer on the lonely moor!"

43 *Chatterton*: The brief, tragic life of poet Thomas Chatterton (1752–1770)
appealed to Wordsworth's imagination. Unable to support himself by
drudging with his pen, Chatterton killed himself in a London garret at the
age of seventeen.   45–46 *Of him . . . mountainside*: another poet who died
young, Robert Burns (1759–1796). It was said that Burns's death had been
hastened by strenuous farm work during his early years.   100 *leeches*:
aquatic blood-sucking worms used by doctors to bleed patients.

269

The Drunk in the Furnace

          For a good decade
The furnace stood in the naked gully, fireless
And vacant as any hat. Then when it was
No more to them than a hulking black fossil
To erode unnoticed with the rest of the junk-hill
By the poisonous creek, and rapidly to be added
          To their ignorance.

          They were afterwards astonished
To confirm, one morning, a twist of smoke like a pale
Resurrection, staggering out of its chewed hole,
And to remark then other tokens that someone,
Cosily bolted behind the eye-holed iron
Door of the drafty burner, had there established
          His bad castle.

          Where he gets his spirits
It's a mystery. But the stuff keeps him musical:
Hammer-and-anvilling with poker and bottle
To his jugged bellowings, till the last groaning clang
As he collapses onto the rioting
Springs of a litter of car-seats ranged on the grates,
          To sleep like an iron pig.

          In their tar-paper church
On a text about stoke-holes that are sated never
Their Reverend lingers. They nod and hate trespassers.
When the furnace wakes, though, all afternoon
Their witless offspring flock like piped rats to its siren
Crescendo, and agape on the crumbling ridge
          Stand in a row and learn.

270

Western Wind

Western wind, when wilt thou blow
The small rain down can rain?
Christ, if my love were in my arms,
And I in my bed again!

2 *The:* so that the.

Divorce

After breakfast and you'd left for school
your mother would call "Come look." What she meant
was sunlight across walnut table tops,
on our painted mantel and the dark floor
and the Bukhara's reds — striking its fringe,
lighting pale damask stripes and a pillow
in blueberry, her favorite blue.

She waited there in a robe also touched
by sun (frailest silk, purple to the floor).
"Come look." From the kitchen I'd come to smile
beside her at this shining of the things
she'd chosen to shine and, putting my hand
on her robe, and would feel the casual nude jolt
from the place I touched through to. And smelled
the original brightness of her hair.

Enough memories tempt me to imagine
what was bearable was better than it was,
whereas the cure between man and wife can
happen the way a pained mind brings to light
wrong habits to learn what's good for a change
without quite forgiving who did it harm.
So, I've come to believe that blame is smart.

I witness this end of the living room,
her things, on the bright mornings of my life
as if she has died, and am less than half
in love with a marriage that both abused
yet held to in solemn faith till those scenes,
the old-fashioned rending of flesh from flesh.
When she recalls me, I suppose she must
manage to with that reflex of some blame
the guilty visit on their counterparts.
Healthy, clear-headed, steadfast distant blame.

Still, I wish her the clichés she needed
to come true, come smoothly true at last.
I wish her a prosperous amnesia
clear as early sun to light up the paint
and belongings in her new husband's place.
I wish her complacency: the good luck
of not having had to admit much since then.
And ease from the destroyer that used to
rage inside her wifeliness, that we all felt
but she most close and helplessly while you three
spent your childhoods in this house left almost
as she left it and kept for you. And her.

35

40

The Snow Man

One must have a mind of winter
To regard the frost and the boughs
Of the pinetrees crusted with snow;

And have been cold a long time
To behold the junipers shagged with ice,
The spruces rough in the distant glitter

Of the January sun; and not to think
Of any misery in the sound of the wind,
In the sound of a few leaves,

Which is the sound of the land
Full of the same wind
That is blowing in the same bare place

For the listener, who listens in the snow,
And, nothing himself, beholds
Nothing that is not there and the nothing that is.

11. Eternal Summer
Loving

Shall I compare thee to a summer's day?

Shall I compare thee to a summer's day?
Thou art more lovely and more temperate.
Rough winds do shake the darling buds of May,
And summer's lease hath all too short a date.
Sometime too hot the eye of heaven shines,
And often is his gold complexion dimmed;
And every fair from fair sometime declines,
By chance, or nature's changing course, untrimmed.
But thy eternal summer shall not fade,
Nor lose possession of that fair thou ow'st;
Nor shall death brag thou wand'rest in his shade,
When in eternal lines to time thou grow'st.
    So long as men can breathe or eyes can see,
    So long lives this, and this gives life to thee.

10 *ow'st:* ownest, has.

Love Poem

The black biplane crashes into the window
of the luncheonette. The pilot climbs down
removing his leather hood.
He hands me my grandmother's jade ring.
No, it is two robin's eggs
and a telephone number: yours.

The Garden of Love

I went to the Garden of Love,
And saw what I never had seen:
A Chapel was built in the midst,
Where I used to play on the green.

And the gates of this Chapel were shut,
And "Thou shalt not" writ over the door;
So I turn'd to the Garden of Love,
That so many sweet flowers bore,

And I saw it was filled with graves,
And tomb-stones where flowers should be:
And priests in black gowns were walking their rounds,
And binding with briars my joys and desires.

I cannot live with You

I cannot live with You –
It would be Life –
And Life is over there –
Behind the Shelf

5   The Sexton keeps the Key to –
Putting up
Our Life – His Porcelain –
Like a Cup –

Discarded of the Housewife –
10   Quaint – or Broke –
A newer Sevres pleases –
Old Ones crack –

I could not die – with You –
For One must wait
15   To shut the Other's Gaze down –
You – could not –

And I – Could I stand by
And see You – freeze –
Without my Right of Frost –
20   Death's privilege?

Nor could I rise – with You –
Because Your Face
Would put out Jesus' –
That New Grace

25   Grow plain – and foreign
On my homesick Eye –
Except that You than He
Shone closer by –

They'd judge Us – How –
30   For You – served Heaven – You know,
Or sought to –
I could not –

Because You saturated Sight –
And I had no more Eyes
35 For sordid excellence
As Paradise

And were You lost, I would be –
Though My Name
Rang loudest
40 On the Heavenly fame –

And were You – saved –
And I – condemned to be
Where You were not –
That self – were Hell to Me –

45 So We must meet apart –
You there – I – here –
With just the Door ajar
That Oceans are – and Prayer –
And that White Sustenance –
50 Despair –

11 *Sevres*: a fine French porcelain.

283

Air is ✓

thinner now
we are together
on the mountain
we feel it
5   crisp
walking on leaves
pine needles
and rocks
where trees
10   are down
the snow
remains
more patient
than I
15   for waiting
is endless
to reach
with you

timberline.

In a Field

Here, in a field
Of devil's paintbrushes,
The circle of far trees
Tightens, and near bushes
Hump like ruins
When the moon floats loosely
Past the desolation
Owl moans wake. Here,
As if the world's
Last lovers, we
Have rung from the ruins
The whippoorwill's
Thrust of melody.
You have fallen asleep,
Breathing as the wind breathes
Among the wetted thistle,
The scented vine,
And, listening, I move
My body toward you,
When a small convulsion
Shakes your hand,
The moonlight flashes
On your teeth.
I am afraid to kiss you.
Never have I wished more
Not to die.

Laboratory Poem

Charles used to watch Naomi, taking heart
And a steel saw, open up turtles, live.
While she swore they felt nothing, he would gag
At blood, at the blind twitching, even after
5   The murky dawn of entrails cleared, revealing
Contours he knew, egg-yellows like lamps paling.

Well then. She carried off the beating heart
To the kymograph and rigged it there, a rag
In fitful wind, now made to strain, now stopped
10   By her solutions tonic or malign
Alternately in which it would be steeped.
What the heart bore, she noted on a chart,

For work did not stop only with the heart.
He thought of certain human hearts, their climb
15   Through violence into exquisite disciplines
Of which, as it now appeared, they all expired.
Soon she would fetch another and start over,
Easy in the presence of her lover.

Location

Always your body like a foreign country
seen in a film and partly understood —
in which an elephant destroys a man
who saw it only in his trophy case,
and the man lies helpless, crushed; in which are seen
the broken bones as fragments of the whole,
and the whole is more than is seen and understood
when the elephant charges with noise, the man screams,
and against an exotic background birds fly;
but always in which, on studio location,
a camera functions as an eye, and somewhere
a man behind it knows the way around —
always your body like a foreign country
teases me out beyond its boundaries,
that vague and very strange geography;
and what eye pierces through the allotted time,
these near, immediate thickets where we hide?

To His Coy Mistress

Had we but world enough, and time,
This coyness, lady, were no crime.
We would sit down and think which way
To walk, and pass our long love's day.
Thou by the Indian Ganges' side
Should'st rubies find; I by the tide
Of Humber would complain. I would
Love you ten years before the Flood,
And you should, if you please, refuse
Till the conversion of the Jews.
My vegetable love should grow
Vaster than empires, and more slow.
An hundred years should go to praise
Thine eyes, and on thy forehead gaze,
Two hundred to adore each breast,
But thirty thousand to the rest.
An age at least to every part,
And the last age should show your heart.
For, lady, you deserve this state,
Nor would I love at lower rate.
   But at my back I always hear
Time's winged chariot hurrying near;
And yonder all before us lie
Deserts of vast eternity.
Thy beauty shall no more be found,
Nor in thy marble vault shall sound
My echoing song; then worms shall try
That long preserved virginity,
And your quaint honor turn to dust,
And into ashes all my lust.
The grave's a fine and private place,
But none, I think, do there embrace.
   Now therefore, while the youthful hue
Sits on thy skin like morning glew,
And while thy willing soul transpires
At every pore with instant fires,
Now let us sport us while we may;

And now, like am'rous birds of prey,
Rather at once our time devour,
Than languish in his slow-chapped power,
Let us roll all our strength, and all
Our sweetness, up into one ball;
And tear our pleasures with rough strife
Thorough the iron gates of life.
Thus, though we cannot make our sun
Stand still, yet we will make him run.

40

45

2 *coyness:* modesty, reluctance.   7 *Humber:* a river that flows by Marvell's town of Hull (on the side of the world opposite from the Ganges); *complain:* sing sad songs.   10 *conversion . . . Jews:* according to St. John the Divine, an event to take place just before the end of the world.   11 *vegetable:* vegetative, flourishing.   34 *glew:* glow.   36 *instant:* eager.
44 *Thorough:* through.

The Flea

Mark but this flea, and mark in this
How little that which thou deny'st me is;
It sucked me first, and now sucks thee,
And in this flea our two bloods mingled be;
Thou know'st that this cannot be said
A sin, nor shame, nor loss of maidenhead,
    Yet this enjoys before it woo,
    And pampered swells with one blood made of two,
    And this, alas, is more than we would do.

Oh stay, three lives in one flea spare,
Where we almost, yea more than married are.
This flea is you and I, and this
Our marriage bed, and marriage temple is;
Though parents grudge, and you, we're met
And cloistered in these living walls of jet.
    Though use make you apt to kill me,
    Let not to that, self-murder added be,
    And sacrilege, three sins in killing three.

Cruel and sudden, hast thou since
Purpled thy nail in blood of innocence?
Wherein could this flea guilty be,
Except in that drop it sucked from thee?
Yet thou triumph'st, and say'st that thou
Find'st not thyself, nor me, the weaker now;
    'Tis true; then learn how false, fears be;
    Just so much honor, when thou yield'st to me,
    Will waste, as this flea's death took life from thee.

16 *use*: custom.

Her Dwarf

Her dwarf at the door bangs and bellows.
She opens — pats him — he tumbles to her.
"O duck!" he roars. "Sweet duckarooney!
Unclench those shoulders and tickle my ears!"
He burrows his head, butts, and pinches.
She balks at his tug.

"Snuggle me, bunny!" he woos her, basso.
"My legs are stubs, but my heart is huge!"
He summers a sault, ramps, then plunges.
"You guzzle me, gosling! Ho ho I can!
Come to the table, and heft me higher!
I'll rumple your silk!"

"Gently," she begs him, "great heart, gently."
He struts his head back and hoots from her haunch.
He shoves the table; she makes him mount it.
"I'm at you, pigeon!" She spreads her arms.
He runs; jumps; pummels. "Oh, huggle me, bear-boy!"
He brays like a man.

I Saw in Louisiana a Live-Oak Growing

I saw in Louisiana a live-oak growing,
All alone stood it and the moss hung down from the branches,
Without any companion it grew there uttering joyous leaves
    of dark green,
And its look, rude, unbending, lusty, made me think of myself,
But I wonder'd how it could utter joyous leaves standing
    alone there without its friend near, for I knew I could not,
And I broke off a twig with a certain number of leaves upon it,
    and twined around it a little moss,
And brought it away, and I have placed it in sight in my room,
It is not needed to remind me as of my own dear friends,
(For I believe lately I think of little else than of them,)
Yet it remains to me a curious token, it makes me think of
    manly love;
For all that, and though the live-oak glistens there in Louisiana
    solitary in a wide flat space,
Uttering joyous leaves all its life without a friend a lover near,
I know very well I could not.

Devouring Time, blunt thou the lion's paws

Devouring Time, blunt thou the lion's paws,
And make the earth devour her own sweet brood;
Pluck the keen teeth from the fierce tiger's jaws,
And burn the long-lived phoenix in her blood;
Make glad and sorry seasons as thou fleets,
And do whate'er thou wilt, swift-footed Time,
To the wide world and all her fading sweets;
But I forbid thee one most heinous crime:
Oh, carve not with thy hours my love's fair brow,
Nor draw no lines there with thine antique pen;
Him in thy course untainted do allow
For beauty's pattern to succeeding men.
Yet do thy worst, old Time. Despite thy wrong,
My love shall in my verse ever live young.

Maratea Porto:
Saying Goodbye to the Vitolos

Should I say, my people? I turned stone
against them long ago, the soupy pictures
of Christ, the crosses drugstores sell.
Cruelty that often goes with stone
makes men virginal or wrong. Outside
the sea has always beat against the rock,
the spray hung passionate, the local bell
sent word of worms to fat fish miles away.

I'm so American, embarrassed by their tears.
Don't they know the saint's bones, high
above us on the mountain, now mean nothing,
and goodbye is common now that love
is just a verb, active as the tide? Why
is Jesus bleeding in that photo on the wall
except to tell the world, when I'm gone
going will be fun? The bright day off the sea
dazzles the flies. Mad purple flies
around me, glint and sizzle and the shaking sea,
the mountain shaking and the saint's bones
raining through the spray, bells gone stale
and money low and this: last days in Italy.
I stand so still. My legs must be diseased.

I forgot my people long ago, reduced them
to some words and wrote their stones away.
Sea slants off their tears with light
no one should forget. I'm still American.
See, afraid to cry. How awkwardly I lean
to kiss them and how suddenly I say
good luck in cracked Italian as I turn my face.

I Knew a Woman

I knew a woman, lovely in her bones,
When small birds sighed, she would sigh back at them;
Ah, when she moved, she moved more ways than one:
The shapes a bright container can contain!
Of her choice virtues only gods should speak,
Or English poets who grew up on Greek
(I'd have them sing in chorus, cheek to cheek).

How well her wishes went! She stroked my chin,
She taught me Turn, and Counter-turn, and Stand;
She taught me Touch, that undulant white skin;
I nibbled meekly from her proffered hand;
She was the sickle; I, poor I, the rake,
Coming behind her for her pretty sake
(But what prodigious mowing we did make).

Love likes a gander, and adores a goose:
Her full lips pursed, the errant note to seize;
She played it quick, she played it light and loose;
My eyes, they dazzled at her flowing knees;
Her several parts could keep a pure repose,
Or one hip quiver with a mobile nose
(She moved in circles, and those circles moved).

Let seed be grass, and grass turn into hay:
I'm martyr to a motion not my own;
What's freedom for? To know eternity.
I swear she cast a shadow white as stone.
But who would count eternity in days?
These old bones live to learn her wanton ways:
(I measure time by how a body sways).

295

Love Poem

Six o'clock and
the sun rises across the river.
The traffic cop wakes up and
crawls over his wife.
The naked professor will sleep another hour.
The dentist wakes up and reaches for a smoke.
The doctor reaches for the phone
and prescribes
his voice full of rust.
The shoeclerk wakes to his clock
touches himself
and lies listening to his woman in the shower.

It is midnight now in Samoa.

Nine o'clock and
the school bell rings.
Miss Gardner taps her ruler on the desk.
She calls the roll.
Oscar Carpenter is absent.
He does not like the sound of the ruler.

It is midnight now in Osaka.

Eleven o'clock:
The salesman makes his way past dogs and wheels
his knuckles already sore
hoping for bells
On Maple Street the policeman's wife
shuts her kimono slowly and shuts the door.
On Willow Street the professor's wife
tells him about her cousin in Mineral Wells
who was also a salesman but never amounted to much.
On Juniper Street the dentist's wife
is drunk and lets him have her on the floor
says she will get a divorce
says she will see him again of course if she can.

It is midnight now in Djakarta.

296

35 Five o'clock and
    the men are coming home.
    The traffic cop comes home
    his ears in his pockets.
    The doctor comes home
40 the sun slipping down his forehead.
    The shoeclerk comes
    The uncertain knees
    still fitting the sockets of his eyes.

    It is midnight now in Berlin.

45 Six o'clock:
    The streetlights come on.

    It is midnight now in Bordeaux.

    Ten o'clock:
    In Mercy Hospital a man is dying.
50 His brain
    squeezes all his thoughts to one thought
    squeezes that to nothing
    and lets go.

    It is midnight now in La Paz.

55 Eleven o'clock:
    The children are gone to bed and we are here
    sitting across the room from one another
    accustomed to this house
    that is not ours to keep
60 to this world that is not ours
    and to each other.

    Sands run through the children in their sleep.

L'Elisir d'Amore

You'd think that at 3:00 A.M.
　　you could take
A nice quiet crap.
The bars are dead;
5　　　juke boxes nod.
The city dreams a smog
　　in which research is an owl
　　　that drifts about in dead smells.
But it never fails.
10 As soon as you settle down
　　your daughter yells
And you wipe, partially, and run
　　up the stairs
To tell her that the blue fox
15　　she saw running through her hair
　　　was choked with laughter
　　　and the peacock in his mouth
　　　was on a Sunday ride and loved it.
To comfort her and send her
20　　back to never-never land
You give her a pat on the ass
And a glass
　　of warm and oily
　　　Cincinnati water.

The title (also that of an opera by Donizetti) means "love potion."

I Hid My Love

I hid my love when young while I
Couldn't bear the buzzing of a fly;
I hid my love to my despite
Till I could not bear to look at light:
I dare not gaze upon her face
But left her memory in each place;
Where'er I saw a wild flower lie
I kissed and bade my love goodbye.

I met her in the greenest dells,
Where dewdrops pearl the wood bluebells;
The lost breeze kissed her bright blue eye,
The bee kissed and went singing by,
A sunbeam found a passage there,
A gold chain round her neck so fair;
As secret as the wild bee's song,
She lay there all the summer long.

I hid my love in field and town
Till e'en the breeze would knock me down;
The bees seemed singing ballads o'er,
The fly's buzz turned a lion's roar;
And even silence found a tongue
To haunt me all the summer long;
The riddle nature could not prove
Was nothing else but secret love.

Love

Love bade me welcome; yet my soul drew back,
    Guilty of dust and sin.
But quick-eyed Love, observing me grow slack
    From my first entrance in,
5   Drew nearer to me, sweetly questioning
    If I lacked anything.

"A guest," I answered, "worthy to be here";
    Love said, "You shall be he."
"I, the unkind, ungrateful? Ah, my dear,
10   I cannot look on Thee."
Love took my hand, and smiling did reply,
    "Who made the eyes but I?"

"Truth, Lord, but I have marred them; let my shame
    Go where it doth deserve."
15   "And know you not," says Love, "who bore the blame?"
    "My dear, then I will serve."
"You must sit down," says Love, "and taste My meat."
    So I did sit and eat.

and spoke: *coopers, craftsmen, shepherds*
blessed is the prophet
whose blood speaks in his stead. Search death out

and sought death in their cities, and was taken
young years and all, and composed in ground
like wintering bees

and after respite stood again
to show in tremendous mime — shut doors sprung,
permeable world, — all man would come to.

La Figlia Che Piange

O quam te memorem virgo . . .

Stand on the highest pavement of the stair —
Lean on a garden urn —
Weave, weave the sunlight in your hair —
Clasp your flowers to you with a pained surprise —
5   Fling them to the ground and turn
With a fugitive resentment in your eyes:
But weave, weave the sunlight in your hair.

   So I would have had him leave,
So I would have had her stand and grieve,
10   So he would have left
As the soul leaves the body torn and bruised,
As the mind deserts the body it has used.
I should find
Some way incomparably light and deft,
15   Some way we both should understand,
Simple and faithless as a smile and shake of the hand.

   She turned away, but with the autumn weather
Compelled my imagination many days,
Many days and many hours:
20   Her hair over her arms and her arms full of flowers.
And I wonder how they should have been together!
I should have lost a gesture and a pose.
Sometimes these cogitations still amaze
The troubled midnight and the noon's repose.

The title means "girl crying." *O quam te memorem virgo . . .* : "What name shall I give you, O maiden?" — the words of Aeneas to his mother and protectress, the goddess Venus, on meeting her in disguise (Virgil, *Aeneid*, Book Two, line 327).

12. As Long as Forever Is

Enduring

Twenty-four years

Twenty-four years remind the tears of my eyes.
(Bury the dead for fear that they walk to the grave in labor.)
In the groin of the natural doorway I crouched like a tailor
Sewing a shroud for a journey
By the light of the meat-eating sun.
Dressed to die, the sensual strut begun,
With my red veins full of money,
In the final direction of the elementary town
I advance for as long as forever is.

as freedom is a breakfastfood

as freedom is a breakfastfood
or truth can live with right and wrong
or molehills are from mountains made
— long enough and just so long
will being pay the rent of seem
and genius please the talentgang
and water most encourage flame

as hatracks into peachtrees grow
or hopes dance best on bald men's hair
and every finger is a toe
and any courage is a fear
— long enough and just so long
will the impure think all things pure
and hornets wail by children stung

or as the seeing are the blind
and robins never welcome spring
nor flatfolk prove their world is round
nor dingsters die at break of dong
and common's rare and millstones float
— long enough and just so long
tomorrow will not be too late

worms are the words but joy's the voice
down shall go which and up come who
breasts will be breasts thighs will be thighs
deeds cannot dream what dreams can do
— time is a tree(this life one leaf)
but love is the sky and i am for you
just so long and long enough

England in 1819

An old, mad, blind, despised, and dying king —
Princes, the dregs of their dull race, who flow
Through public scorn — mud from a muddy spring;
Rulers who neither see, nor feel, nor know,
But leechlike to their fainting country cling,
Till they drop, blind in blood, without a blow;
A people starved and stabbed in the untilled field —
An army, which liberticide and prey
Makes as a two-edged sword to all who wield;
Golden and sanguine laws which tempt and slay;
Religion Christless, Godless — a book sealed;
A Senate — Time's worst statute unrepealed —
Are graves, from which a glorious Phantom may
Burst, to illumine our tempestuous day.

1 *An old . . . king*: George III, senile and insane for the previous nine years.   10 *Golden and sanguine laws*: those passed for love of money and resulting in bloodshed.   12 *Time's worst statute*: probably the Test Act, curbing the rights of Irish Roman Catholics.   13 *Phantom*: liberty? the spirit of revolution?

A Very Old Woman

Climbs hobbling
rocky path, gnarled
bougainvillea twist
from pot-holed earth
round & above
her head lurching
past cacti, shrubs
growing without
rain like her, poking
with her shiny
walking-stick cold
spring air, sun
winding in her
black velvet dress her
moustache wet her
face of a manytime
opened leather sack
one black tooth shaking
from blond lips
doesn't care about
bees, hum of
death but
pushes against sun
blood-brown
sun like a girder
on her gristle
past muffle of
wave-lap, child
shriek up
rock-crusted hill
stumbles slow hands
for a vine &
flat rib flat
one hand on a
stone one
hand on a

                    stone one foot
                    on a stone one
                    foot on a stone &
40   up
                    with fire in her eyes
                    to beat that sun
                    to top of hill
                    whops the ground
45   with her walking-
                    stick, curses sun
                    body climbing
                    through nettles
                    webs, thorns
50   shale sliding
                    under her feet
                    light wound in
                    night-black dress
                    measuring her way
55   to sharp of the
                    wall rock
                    rock rock rock
                    rock & through to
                    wind-raw crest
60   hunched & fragrant
                    shapes, sail shapes
                    black in the rolling
                    cloud sky, moving
                    from stone to tree
65   to wood to
                    rock
                    to find the plot
                    & place her crushed
                    stemmed flower
70   at the cross's
                    foot

                    Chapala, Mexico, 1959

                    311

How to Be Old

It is easy to be young. (Everybody is,
at first.) It is not easy
to be old. It takes time.
Youth is given; age is achieved.
5   One must work a magic to mix with time
in order to become old.

Youth is given. One must put it away
like a doll in a closet,
take it out and play with it only
10   on holidays. One must have many dresses
and dress the doll impeccably
(but not to show the doll, to keep it hidden.)

It is necessary to adore the doll,
to remember it in the dark on the ordinary
15   days, and every day congratulate
one's aging face in the mirror.

In time one will be very old.
In time, one's life will be accomplished.
And in time, in time, the doll —
20   like new, though ancient — will be found.

Seven of "The Ten-Fifteen
Community Poems"

she says how
is it when you
speak in front of
the assembly
the holy
ghost puts his
foot in your mouth

i say why
dont you iron my
shirt

     *

anger wrenches
the womb the child
squalls in the air
now the man
fleshed
strangles on the word

what is it
we have done

     *

blue stars
of small blue
flowers

periwinkle

prayer rugs
tied with a thousand
knots

no one
will unravel them

     *

the night is good

mockingbirds
30   kindle an incense
of the hours

i know
that in such a darkness
a man should walk
35   in his sandals

                    *

in all this yesterday
where am I

the fig tree would not bloom

and now the elections
40   hook the bodies of officials
and drag them up
from vats of formaldehyde

the priest is lonely

he uncovers his chalice
45   for a drop of rain

                    *

we come
from sleep

creation begins
and the light
50   comes slowly on

we hear his voice

share me
and be still
be still now

                    *

55 I stretch out my hand
who will touch it

my fingers
circle the wind

if I dont know who I am
60 the wind does

The seven poems have been excerpted from a longer sequence, published as a booklet in 1971. Asked about his work, John Knoepfle commented: "The ten-fifteen community is just the name for the group that celebrates a liturgy together on Sundays at that time. The poems are interesting to me because I was trying to write within the sensibility of that association, and not out of my own ego."

Ode on Melancholy

1

No, no, go not to Lethe, neither twist
    Wolfsbane, tight-rooted, for its poisonous wine;
Nor suffer thy pale forehead to be kissed
    By nightshade, ruby grape of Proserpine;
5   Make not your rosary of yew-berries,
      Nor let the beetle, nor the death-moth be
        Your mournful Psyche, nor the downy owl
A partner in your sorrow's mysteries;
    For shade to shade will come too drowsily,
10   And drown the wakeful anguish of the soul.

2

But when the melancholy fit shall fall
    Sudden from heaven like a weeping cloud,
That fosters the droop-headed flowers all,
    And hides the green hill in an April shroud;
15   Then glut thy sorrow on a morning rose,
      Or on the rainbow of the salt sand-wave,
      Or on the wealth of globèd peonies;
Or if thy mistress some rich anger shows,
    Imprison her soft hand, and let her rave,
20   And feed deep, deep upon her peerless eyes.

3

She dwells with Beauty — Beauty that must die;
  And Joy, whose hand is ever at his lips
Bidding adieu; and aching Pleasure nigh,
  Turning to Poison while the bee-mouth sips.
25 Aye, in the very temple of Delight
  Veiled Melancholy has her sov'reign shrine,
    Though seen of none save him whose strenuous tongue
  Can burst Joy's grape against his palate fine;
His soul shall taste the sadness of her might,
30   And be among her cloudy trophies hung.

1 *Lethe*: river in Hades. In Greek mythology dead souls, drinking from its waters, forget the living. 2, 4 *Wolfsbane, nightshade*: poisonous herbs, sources of drugs used as sedatives. Nightshade might kiss the lady's forehead because, under the name belladonna, it was used as a cosmetic.
4 *Proserpine*: queen of the underworld. 5 *yew-berries*: Yew trees were favorite graveyard plants, conventional symbols of mourning. 6, 7 *beetle, death-moth, owl*: In folk superstition, the clicking of a beetle, the passage of a death's-head moth (so called because its markings look like a skull), and the hooting of an owl were thought omens of someone's death. 7 *Psyche*: the soul. According to one legend, when a person dies, his soul in the form of a moth creeps forth from his lips and flies away.

The World Is Too Much with Us

The world is too much with us; late and soon,
Getting and spending, we lay waste our powers:
Little we see in Nature that is ours;
We have given our hearts away, a sordid boon!
5 This Sea that bares her bosom to the moon;
The winds that will be howling at all hours,
And are up-gathered now like sleeping flowers;
For this, for everything, we are out of tune;
It moves us not. — Great God! I'd rather be
10 A pagan suckled in a creed outworn;
So might I, standing on this pleasant lea,
Have glimpses that would make me less forlorn;
Have sight of Proteus rising from the sea;
Or hear old Triton blow his wreathèd horn.

If I Could Only Live at the
Pitch That Is Near Madness

If I could only live at the pitch that is near madness
When everything is as it was in my childhood
Violent, vivid, and of infinite possibility:
That the sun and the moon broke over my head.

Then I cast time out of the trees and fields,
Then I stood immaculate in the Ego;
Then I eyed the world with all delight,
Reality was the perfection of my sight.

And time has big handles on the hands,
Fields and trees a way of being themselves.
I saw battalions of the race of mankind
Standing stolid, demanding a moral answer.

I gave the moral answer and I died
And into a realm of complexity came
Where nothing is possible but necessity
And the truth wailing there like a red babe.

When I consider how my light is spent

When I consider how my light is spent,
    Ere half my days in this dark world and wide,
    And that one talent which is death to hide
    Lodged with me useless, though my soul more bent
5   To serve therewith my Maker, and present
    My true account, lest He returning chide;
    "Doth God exact day-labor, light denied?"
    I fondly ask. But Patience, to prevent
That murmur, soon replies, "God doth not need
10   Either man's work or His own gifts. Who best
    Bear His mild yoke, they serve Him best. His state
Is kingly: thousands at His bidding speed,
    And post o'er land and ocean without rest;
    They also serve who only stand and wait."

1–2 *my light . . . my days*: Milton had become blind before he was fifty
(when half his life was spent out of a possible hundred years). 3 *that one*
talent: For Christ's parable of the talents (measures of money), see Matthew
25:14–30. 8 *fondly*: foolishly.

320

The Pleasures of Merely Circulating

The garden flew round with the angel,
The angel flew round with the clouds,
And the clouds flew round and the clouds flew round
And the clouds flew round with the clouds.

5   Is there any secret in skulls,
The cattle skulls in the woods?
Do the drummers in black hoods
Rumble anything out of their drums?

Mrs. Anderson's Swedish baby
10 Might well have been German or Spanish,
Yet that things go round and again go round
Has rather a classical sound.

Bruckner

In the dark aisles of Bruckner's symphonies
The Katzenjammer Kids are moving.
They come tumbling down the harp arpeggios
Into the heavy somber chords.
5   Bouncing off the brass crescendi
They are putting glue under the violins,
Twicking the tuning knobs of the cellos, and
Hans, now, has slyly placed a firecracker
In the bell of the bulbous tuba.
10   As usual they are playing tricks on the Captain
And golden-haired Rollo, the English boy,
Who, jointly, for these two are conspirators,
Call loudly for Mamma.
While in one apocalyptic burst of sound
15   Thousands of angels waving thousands of palms
Around one great celestial light,
And a pitiful old man addresses the Emperor, asking,
"Please don't let them make fun of my music."

The Austrian composer and organist Anton Bruckner (1824–1896) flourished
during the reign of Emperor Franz Joseph I.

America

America, you ode for reality!
Give back the people you took.

Let the sun shine again
on the four corners of the world

5   you thought of first but do not
own, or keep like a convenience.

People are your own word, you
invented that locus and term.

Here, you said and say, is
10   where we are. Give back

what we are, these people you made,
us, and nowhere but you to be.

Sunflower Sutra

I walked on the banks of the tincan banana dock and sat
   down under the huge shade of a Southern Pacific locomo-
   tive to look at the sunset over the box house hills and cry.
Jack Kerouac sat beside me on a busted rusty iron pole,
   companion, we thought the same thoughts of the soul,
   bleak and blue and sad-eyed, surrounded by the gnarled
   steel roots of trees of machinery.
The oily water on the river mirrored the red sky, sun sank on
   top of final Frisco peaks, no fish in that stream, no hermit
   in those mounts, just ourselves rheumy-eyed and hung-
   over like those old bums on the riverbank, tired and wily.
Look at the Sunflower, he said, there was a dead gray shadow
   against the sky, big as a man, sitting dry on top of a pile
   of ancient sawdust —
— I rushed up enchanted — it was my first sunflower, mem-
   ories of Blake — my visions — Harlem
and Hells of the Eastern rivers, bridges clanking Joes Greasy
   Sandwiches, dead baby carriages, black treadless tires
   forgotten and unretreaded, the poem of the riverbank,
   condoms & pots, steel knives, nothing stainless, only the
   dank muck and the razor sharp artifacts passing into the
   past —
and the gray Sunflower poised against the sunset, crackly
   bleak and dusty with the smut and smog and smoke of
   olden locomotives in its eye —
corolla of bleary spikes pushed down and broken like a bat-
   tered crown, seeds fallen out of its face, soon-to-be-
   toothless mouth of sunny air, sunrays obliterated on its
   hairy head like a dried wire spiderweb,
leaves stuck out like arms out of the stem, gestures from the
   sawdust root, broke pieces of plaster fallen out of the
   black twigs, a dead fly in its ear,
Unholy battered old thing you were, my sunflower O my
   soul, I loved you then!
The grime was no man's grime but death and human locomo-
   tives,

324

all that dress of dust, that veil of darkened railroad skin, that
smog of cheek, that eyelid of black mis'ry, that sooty
hand or phallus or protuberance of artificial worse-than-
dirt — industrial — modern — all that civilization spot-
ting your crazy golden crown —
and those blear thoughts of death and dusty loveless eyes and
ends and withered roots below, in the home-pile of sand
and sawdust, rubber dollar bills, skin of machinery, the
guts and innards of the weeping coughing car, the empty
lonely tincans with their rusty tongues alack, what more
could I name, the smoked ashes of some cock cigar, the
cunts of wheelbarrows and the milky breasts of cars,
wornout asses out of chairs & sphincters of dynamos —
all these
entangled in your mummied roots — and you there standing
before me in the sunset, all your glory in your form!
A perfect beauty of a sunflower! a perfect excellent lovely
sunflower existence! a sweet natural eye to the new hip
moon, woke up alive and excited grasping in the sunset
shadow sunrise golden monthly breeze!
How many flies buzzed round you innocent of your grime
while you cursed the heavens of the railroad and your
flower soul?
Poor dead flower? when did you forget you were a flower?
when did you look at your skin and decide you were an
impotent dirty old locomotive? the ghost of a locomo-
tive? the specter and shade of a once powerful mad
American locomotive?
You were never no locomotive, Sunflower, you were a sun-
flower!
And you Locomotive, you are a locomotive, forget me not!
So I grabbed up the skeleton thick sunflower and stuck it at
my side like a scepter.
and deliver my sermon to my soul, and Jack's soul too, and
anyone who'll listen,
We're not our skin of grime, we're not our dread bleak dusty

325

imageless locomotive, we're all beautiful golden sun-
flowers inside, we're blessed by our own seed & golden
hairy naked accomplishment-bodies growing into mad
black formal sunflowers in the sunset, spied on by our
eyes under the shadow of the mad locomotive riverbank
sunset Frisko hilly tincan evening sitdown vision.

Berkeley 1955

Pepsi Generation

Paper tiger throw H-bomb in south pole
Paper dragon drop A-bomb in north pole
Ice mountains crash
Turn soda
So many water everywhere
Everybody swimming
Day and night
Eat fish

Lapis Lazuli

For Harry Clifton

I have heard that hysterical women say
They are sick of the palette and fiddle-bow,
Of poets that are always gay,
For everybody knows or else should know
That if nothing drastic is done
Aeroplane and Zeppelin will come out,
Pitch like King Billy bomb-balls in
Until the town lie beaten flat.

All perform their tragic play,
There struts Hamlet, there is Lear,
That's Ophelia, that Cordelia;
Yet they, should the last scene be there,
The great stage curtain about to drop,
If worthy their prominent part in the play,
Do not break up their lines to weep.
They know that Hamlet and Lear are gay;
Gaiety transfiguring all that dread.
All men have aimed at, found and lost;
Black out; Heaven blazing into the head:
Tragedy wrought to its uttermost.
Though Hamlet rambles and Lear rages,
And all the drop-scenes drop at once
Upon a hundred thousand stages,
It cannot grow by an inch or an ounce.

On their own feet they came, or on shipboard,
Camel-back, horse-back, ass-back, mule-back,
Old civilizations put to the sword.
Then they and their wisdom went to rack:
No handiwork of Callimachus,
Who handled marble as if it were bronze,
Made draperies that seemed to rise
When sea-wind swept the corner, stands;
His long lamp-chimney shaped like the stem
Of a slender palm, stood but a day;

35 All things fall and are built again,
And those that build them again are gay.

Two Chinamen, behind them a third,
Are carved in lapis lazuli,
Over them flies a long-legged bird,
40 A symbol of longevity;
The third, doubtless a serving-man,
Carries a musical instrument.

Every discoloration of the stone,
Every accidental crack or dent,
45 Seems a water-course or an avalanche,
Or lofty slope where it still snows
Though doubtless plum or cherry-branch
Sweetens the little half-way house
Those Chinamen climb towards, and I
50 Delight to imagine them seated there;
There, on the mountain and the sky,
On all the tragic scene they stare.
One asks for mournful melodies;
Accomplished fingers begin to play.
55 Their eyes mid many wrinkles, their eyes,
Their ancient, glittering eyes, are gay.

Lapis lazuli is a deep blue semi-precious stone; the carving Yeats describes
in lines 37–56 was made from it. 7 *King Billy*: William of Orange, English
king, who used cannon against the Irish in the Battle of the Boyne (1690).
Yeats may also have in mind a modern King Billy: Kaiser Wilhelm II of
Germany, who had sent zeppelins to bomb London in World War I.
29 *Callimachus*: Athenian sculptor, fifth century B.C.

329

Advice to a Prophet

When you come, as you soon must, to the streets of our city,
Mad-eyed from stating the obvious,
Not proclaiming our fall but begging us
In God's name to have self-pity,

5   Spare us all word of the weapons, their force and range,
The long numbers that rocket the mind;
Our slow, unreckoning hearts will be left behind,
Unable to fear what is too strange.

Nor shall you scare us with talk of the death of the race.
10   How should we dream of this place without us? —
The sun mere fire, the leaves untroubled about us,
A stone look on the stone's face?

Speak of the world's own change. Though we cannot conceive
Of an undreamt thing, we know to our cost
How the dreamt cloud crumbles, the vines are blackened
15   by frost,
How the view alters. We could believe,

If you told us so, that the white-tailed deer will slip
Into perfect shade, grown perfectly shy,
The lark avoid the reaches of our eye,
20   The jack-pine lose its knuckled grip

On the cold ledge, and every torrent burn
As Xanthus once, its gliding trout
Stunned in a twinkling. What should we be without
The dolphin's arc, the dove's return,

25   These things in which we have seen ourselves and spoken?
Ask us, prophet, how we shall call
Our natures forth when that live tongue is all
Dispelled, that glass obscured or broken

In which we have said the rose of our love and the clean
30   Horse of our courage, in which beheld
The singing locust of the soul unshelled,
And all we mean or wish to mean.

330

Ask us, ask us whether with the worldless rose
Our hearts shall fail us; come demanding
35   Whether there shall be lofty or long standing
When the bronze annals of the oak-tree close.

In a Dark Time

In a dark time, the eye begins to see,
I meet my shadow in the deepening shade;
I hear my echo in the echoing wood —
A lord of nature weeping to a tree.
I live between the heron and the wren,
Beasts of the hill and serpents of the den.

What's madness but nobility of soul
At odds with circumstance? The day's on fire!
I know the purity of pure despair,
My shadow pinned against a sweating wall.
That place among the rocks — is it a cave,
Or winding path? The edge is what I have.

A steady storm of correspondences!
A night flowing with birds, a ragged moon,
And in broad day the midnight come again!
A man goes far to find out what he is —
Death of the self in a long, tearless night,
All natural shapes blazing unnatural light.

Dark, dark my light, and darker my desire.
My soul, like some heat-maddened summer fly,
Keeps buzzing at the sill. Which I is *I*?
A fallen man, I climb out of my fear.
The mind enters itself, and God the mind,
And one is One, free in the tearing wind.

How Many Nights

How many nights
have I lain in terror,
O Creator Spirit, Maker of night and day,

only to walk out
the next morning over the frozen world
hearing under the creaking of snow
faint, peaceful breaths . . .
snake,
bear, earthworm, ant . . .

and above me
a wild crow crying *'yaw yaw yaw'*
from a branch nothing cried from ever in my life.

Lives of the Poets

with Titles of Books and Record Albums
for Further Reading and Listening

The books listed after each biographical note are all collections of poetry. Selected or collected editions, instead of separate titles, have been listed whenever possible. For major poets of the past, many useful editions may exist in addition to the one recommended.

Helen Adam (born 1909 in Glasgow, Scotland) studied at Edinburgh University and worked as a journalist in London and Edinburgh before coming to America in 1939. She has lived in Reno, Oakland, and San Francisco, and now makes her home in New York City. Besides her ballads, which she occasionally sings in public, Miss Adam has written a play produced off-Broadway, *San Francisco's Burning.*

The Queen o' Crow Castle (1958), *Ballads* (1964), *Counting Out Rhyme* (1972).

A. R. Ammons (born 1926 in Whiteville, North Carolina) was once principal of an elementary school on Cape Hatteras. After nine years in business, as vice-president of a biological glassware firm, he returned to teaching and is a professor at Cornell. Knowledge of science and of North Carolina speech inform his poetry, which includes *Tape for the Turn of the Year* (1965), a poem written on a continuous strip of adding-machine tape.

Collected Poems 1951–1971 (1972).

Matthew Arnold (1822–1888), English poet and critic, was schooled as a boy at Rugby, where his father was headmaster. Most of Arnold's work in poetry was completed early, and he devoted much of his later life to educational reform, spending thirty-six years as a school inspector. He wrote influential essays and lectures championing liberal humanism. Arnold maintained that literature plays an active role in society and argued in his essay on Wordsworth "that poetry is at bottom a criticism of life; that the greatness of a poet lies in his powerful and beautiful application of ideas to life — to the question: How to live."

Poetical Works, ed. C. B. Tinker and H. F. Lowry (1953).

W. H. Auden (born 1907 in York, England) as a young man in the 1930's became the acknowledged spokesman for a generation of English poets that included his friends C. Day Lewis, Christopher Isherwood, and Louis MacNeice. In 1939 Auden came to America and took out citizenship papers. Recently, he returned to England, though he is an American citizen. A prolific editor, anthologist, and translator of poetry, Auden also has collaborated on plays, opera librettos, and travel memoirs. He has written influential criticism, much of it collected in *The Dyer's Hand* (1962).

Collected Shorter Poems 1927–1957 (1967), *Collected Longer Poems* (1969), *City Without Walls* (1970), *Epistle to a Godson* (1972). Record album, *W. H. Auden Reading,* Caedmon, TC 1019.

Stephen Vincent Benét (1898–1943), American poet, novelist, and short-story writer, was born in Bethlehem, Pennsylvania. *John Brown's Body,*

337

a long Civil War poem with many voices, has been given successful theatrical production. Benét's use of folklore and American history is reflected too in several memorable stories, among them "The Devil and Daniel Webster."

John Brown's Body (1928), *Western Star* (1943), *Selected Poetry and Prose* (1960). Record album: *The Poetry of Stephen Vincent Benét Read by the Author and Joseph Wiseman*, Caedmon, TC 1337.

Daniel Berrigan (born 1921 in Virginia, Minnesota) is a Jesuit priest and Lamont Award winning poet well known as a leader of protests against the Vietnam war. One of the Catonsville Nine who poured homemade napalm on draft records in 1968, he was tried and served a federal prison sentence. He wrote a play based on his experience, *The Trial of the Catonsville Nine*, produced in New York and elsewhere. *Night Flight to Hanoi* is his journal of a trip to North Vietnam, where he assisted in obtaining the release of three captured United States airmen.

Time Without Number (1957), *World for Wedding Ring* (1962), *They Call Us Dead Men* (1966), *No One Walks Waters* (1966), *Love, Love at the End* (1968), *False Gods, Real Men* (1969), *Trial Poems* (1970), *No Bars to Manhood* (1970), *Encounters* (1971), *The Dark Night of Resistance* (1971).

Elizabeth Bishop (born 1911 in Worcester, Massachusetts) spent early childhood in a village in Nova Scotia. A graduate of Vassar, she served as Consultant in Poetry for the Library of Congress and for the past three years has been teaching at Harvard. She has published sparingly and has written short fiction as well as poetry. From 1952 to 1970 she made her home in Brazil.

Complete Poems (1969).

William Blake (1757–1827), poet, painter, and visionary, was born in the Soho district of London and was apprenticed to an engraver early in life. He was able to make a living illustrating books, among them Dante's *Divine Comedy*, Milton's poems, and the Book of Job. A remarkable graphic artist, Blake published his own poems, engraving them in careful script, embellished with hand-colored illustrations and decorations. Never afraid to speak his mind and ill famed for his sympathy with the French Revolution, Blake was put on trial for sedition, but the charges were dismissed. With his wife Catherine, a poor girl whom he taught to read and write, Blake shared his visions. In his lifetime, Wordsworth and Coleridge were among the few admirers of his short lyrics; his long "Prophetic Books" have had to wait until our century for sympathetic readers. Out of his readings in alchemy, the Bible, and the works of Plato and Swedenborg, Blake derived support for his lifelong hatred of scientific rationalism and created his own mythology.

Works, ed. Geoffrey Keynes (1957).

Robert Bly (born 1926 in Madison, Minnesota) lives on the farm that was his birthplace. In 1958 he began the influential poetry magazine

The Fifties (now called *The Seventies*), in which he urged American poets to open their work to dream and surrealism and to influences from Europe and Latin America. Bly has translated the poems of Georg Trakl, Pablo Neruda, Juan Ramón Jiménez, César Vallejo, and others. In his poetry and in person he has been an outspoken opponent of the Vietnam war.

Silence in the Snowy Fields (1962), *The Light Around the Body* (1967), *The Teeth Mother Naked at Last* (1971), *Sleepers Joining Hands* (1972).

Louise Bogan (1897–1970) was born in Livermore Falls, Maine. She attended Girls' Latin School in Boston and dropped out of Boston University after her freshman year. The death of her first husband left her with one daughter; later, she was married for a time to the poet Raymond Holden. Most of her life was spent in New York City, where for many years she reviewed poetry books for *The New Yorker*. Her *Selected Criticism* appeared in 1955.

The Blue Estuaries (1968).

Philip Booth (born 1925 in Hanover, New Hampshire) has lived much of his life on the coast of Maine — a landscape reflected especially in his collection of poems *The Islanders* (1961). In World War II he served in the United States air force as a pilot. At present he is professor of English at Syracuse University.

Weathers and Edges (1966), *Margins* (1970).

Anne Bradstreet (1612?–1672), first American woman to be recognized for her poetry, came from England to Massachusetts, where her husband, Simon Bradstreet, twice served as colonial governor. Within her Puritan piety, she was capable of a wide range of feeling, as she demonstrated in her one book, *The Tenth Muse Lately Sprung Up in America* (1650), published in London by friends without her consent.

Poems of Anne Bradstreet, ed. Robert Hutchinson (1969).

Richard Brautigan (born 1935 in Tacoma, Washington) enjoyed an underground reputation as a writer, which abruptly surfaced. His works include the popular anti-novels *Trout Fishing in America, A Confederate General from Big Sur, In Watermelon Sugar*, and *The Abortion*. His *Please Plant This Book* is a collection of poems printed on seed packets. He lives in San Francisco and has a teenage daughter.

The Pill Versus the Springhill Mine Disaster (1968), *Rommel Drives Deep into Egypt* (1970), *Revenge of the Lawn* (1971).

John Michael Brennan (born 1950 in Denver, Colorado) has been studying at Tufts University, playing guitar, and writing songs and poems. His photographs and poems have appeared in *Good Shit, Counter/Measures, mysticriverreader*, and other little magazines. He has won an Academy of American Poets college award and has attended the Bread Loaf Writers Conference on a scholarship.

Air Is (1972).

Emily Brontë (1818–1848), English poet and novelist, grew up in a parsonage on the Yorkshire moors. With her sisters Charlotte and Anne, she turned early to writing, producing a single novel, *Wuthering Heights*.

The Complete Poems of Emily Jane Bronte, ed. C. W. Hatfield (1941).

Gwendolyn Brooks (born 1917 in Topeka, Kansas) came early in life to the South Side of Chicago, whose people she has commemorated in her poetry and in a novel, *Maud Martha*. Recipient of the Pulitzer Prize for poetry in 1950, she has long been recognized as an outstanding voice in modern American black literature.

Selected Poems (1963), *In the Mecca* (1968), *Family Pictures* (1971), *The World of Gwendolyn Brooks* (1971), *Aloneness* (1972).

Robert Browning (1812–1889) was born in Camberwell, a suburb of London, and was educated primarily in his father's large library. In 1846 he eloped to Italy with the poet Elizabeth Barrett; the couple lived in Pisa and Florence until her death in 1861. Browning then returned to England, where he received late but loud applause. A prolific poet, he was the author of a long narrative poem, *The Ring and the Book*, based on an Italian murder trial of the seventeenth century, and he wrote several plays, among them *A Blot in the 'Scutcheon*. Readers have most favored Browning's dramatic monologues, such as "My Last Duchess," in which he frequently brings to new life certain figures of the Italian Renaissance.

The Complete Poetical Works of Robert Browning, ed. Augustine Birrell (1915).

Charles Bukowski (born 1920 in Andernach, Germany) came to the United States as a child and grew up in Los Angeles. A poet with a delayed vocation, Bukowski did not publish his first collection of poetry until he was past forty. He has written a weekly column, "Notes of a Dirty Old Man," for the underground press and is the author of *All the Assholes in the World and Mine*, a history of a hemorrhoid operation.

new and selected poems 1955–63 (1963), *Crucifix in a Deathhand* (1965), *Cold Dogs in the Courtyard* (1965), *At Terror Street and Agony Way* (1968), *Poems Written Before Jumping Out of an 8 Story Window* (1968), *Penguin Modern Poets 13* (with Philip Lamantia and Harold Norse, 1969), *The Days Run Away like Wild Horses over the Hills* (1969), *Mockingbird Wish Me Luck* (1972).

James Camp (born 1923 in Alexandria, Louisiana) served in the army in the South Pacific in World War II and studied at Louisiana State University and the University of Michigan. He has edited or co-edited literary magazines such as *Olivet Quarterly*, *Arbor*, and *Burning Deck* and is an editor of two anthologies, *Mark Twain's Frontier* and *Pegasus Descending: A Book of the Best Bad Verse*. Camp teaches at Newark College of Engineering.

An Edict from the Emperor (1969).

Thomas Campion (1567–1620), Elizabethan courtier and physician, was the author of several books of lute songs much admired for their masterful combination of words and music.

The Works of Thomas Campion, ed. Walter R. Davis (1967).

Hodding Carter (1907–1972), one of the best-known newspapermen in the South, was a native of Hammond, Louisiana. He moved to Greenville, Mississippi, where at the time of his death he was publisher of the *Delta-Democrat Times*. Carter's stand against segregation brought him many local attacks and, in 1946, a Pulitzer Prize for editorial writing. The author of more than a dozen books of history, reportage, and comment, Carter left a single collection of poems.

The Ballad of Catfoot Grimes and Other Verse (1964).

William Childress (born 1933 in Hugo, Oklahoma) spent seven years in the army and Korean war service as a demolitions specialist, then took a B.A. in English from Fresno State College and an M.F.A. from the University of Iowa. His poems have appeared in more than fifty magazines, among them *Harper's, Kenyon Review, The Reporter, Hearse,* and *Westways*. Co-winner of the 1970 Stephen Vincent Benét Award and of the 1971 Devins Award, he is married and has three sons.

Burning the Years (1971), *Lobo* (1972).

John Ciardi (born 1916 in Boston) studied poetry with John Holmes at Tufts University, won a Hopwood writing prize at the University of Michigan, and for many years taught at Harvard and Rutgers. Ciardi has translated the complete *Divine Comedy* of Dante and has written many popular books for children. A busy lecturer and reader of his poetry, he was poetry editor of the *Saturday Review* from 1956 to 1972 and for many years directed the Bread Loaf Writers Conference.

As If, Poems New and Selected (1955), *I Marry You* (1958), *Thirty-nine Poems* (1959), *The Reason for the Pelican* (1959), *In the Stoneworks* (1961), *In Fact* (1962), *Person to Person* (1964), *This Strangest Everything* (1966), *Lives of X* (1970).

John Clare (1793–1864), English poet of rural life, was born in Northamptonshire, the son of a farm worker. His first poems enjoyed a brief vogue, but from 1840 until the end of his life Clare was confined in public mental asylums.

Poems of John Clare, ed. J. W. Tibble (1938), *Poems of John Clare's Madness*, ed. Geoffrey Grigson (1949).

Lucille Clifton (born 1936 in Depew, New York) attended Howard University and New York State College at Fredonia. She now makes her home in Baltimore. She is married, the mother of six, and besides her own poetry has written books for children.

Good Times (1969), *Good News About the Earth* (1972).

Samuel Taylor Coleridge (1772–1834) was born in Devonshire, England. With Wordsworth, he collected his early poems in the *Lyrical Ballads* of 1798, a milestone in the Romantic movement in English literature. Coleridge remains one of the supreme

341

English critics (see his *Biographia Literaria*), as well as a seminal writer on philosophy, theology, and political theory. He struggled against an unhappy marriage, an opium habit, and a tendency toward dejection and triumphed in a few completed poems, among them *The Rime of the Ancient Mariner*.

Poetical Works, ed. E. H. Coleridge (1912).

Gregory Corso (born 1930 in New York City) is recognized, with Allen Ginsberg and the late Jack Kerouac, as a central figure in the Beat literary movement. Corso's early life was spent mostly in foster homes and institutions. In 1955, when he was living in Cambridge, Massachusetts, friendly Harvard students helped publish his first book of poems. His later work includes a novel, *American Express*.

Vestal Lady on Brattle (1955), *Gasoline* (1958), *The Happy Birthday of Death* (1959), *Long Live Man* (1962), *The Mutation of the Spirit*, *A Shuffle Poem* (1964), *Elegaic Feelings American* (1970).

Henri Coulette (born 1927 in Los Angeles) studied in the writers' workshop of the University of Iowa and received the Lamont Award for his first collection. He teaches at California State College in Los Angeles.

The War of the Secret Agents (1965), *The Family Goldschmitt* (1971).

Hart Crane (1899–1932), son of an Ohio candy manufacturer, went to New York City at the age of seventeen, determined to be a poet.

Crane's struggles to support himself, to further his literary career, and to cope with love and alcohol ended in suicide. His roughly finished long poem, *The Bridge*, is highly ambitious and has impressive sections. John Unterecker's *Voyager: A Life of Hart Crane* (1969) is a full recent biography.

Complete Poems and Selected Letters and Prose, ed. Brom Weber (1966).

Stephen Crane (1871–1900), author and newspaperman, was born in Newark, New Jersey, the fourteenth child of a Methodist minister. In *Maggie, A Girl of the Streets* (1893), Crane was an early exponent of naturalism in American fiction. He is probably best known for his psychological novel of the Civil War, *The Red Badge of Courage* (1895). In short stories such as "The Blue Hotel" and "The Open Boat," Crane seems years in advance of his time; so too in his poetry, with its terse irony and open verse form.

Poems, ed. J. Katz (1966).

Robert Creeley (born 1926 in Arlington, Massachusetts) attended Harvard, served in Burma during World War II, lived in France, Spain, and Mexico. He was graduated from Black Mountain College in North Carolina, where he remained as a teacher and as editor of the influential little magazine *Black Mountain Review*. Creeley has written a novel, *The Island*, and a book of stories, *The Gold Diggers*, as well as a collection of reviews and criticism, *A Quick Graph*. He is presently teaching at San Francisco

342

State College. His terse, knotty poems have had great impact upon younger poets.

For Love: Poems 1950–1960 (1962), *Words* (1967), *Pieces* (1969), *The Charm: Early and Uncollected Poems* (1970), *A Day Book* (1972).

Victor Hernandez Cruz (born 1949 in Aguas Buenas, Puerto Rico) came to New York City in 1954 and attended Benjamin Franklin High School. He has been an editor of *Umbra*, a magazine of black culture and poetry, and has worked with the Gut Theater in New York.

Papo Got His Gun (1966), *Snaps* (1969).

E. E. Cummings (1894–1962) was born in Cambridge, Massachusetts, son of a minister, and studied classics at Harvard. Through his long career as poet, playwright, and painter, Cummings affirmed the worth of the individual. Mistakenly arrested and confined to a French prison while serving as an ambulance driver in World War I, Cummings embodied the experience in his novel *The Enormous Room* (1922). His lyric poems sometimes revel in typographical experiment but in themes and sentiment are often more conventional than they appear.

Collected Poems (1963), *Three Plays and a Ballet*, ed. George J. Firmage (1967). Record album: *E. E. Cummings Reading His Poetry*, Caedmon, TC 1017.

Waring Cuney (born 1906 in Washington, D.C.), whose full name is William Waring Cuney, was educated in Washington public schools and at Howard University in the same city. While a freshman at Howard he wrote "No Images," a poem that won a first prize in an *Opportunity* contest two years later. During World War II he served as a technical sergeant; "O.T.'s Blues" was written after his return to civilian life. At present he lives in New York City.

Puzzles (1960).

J. V. Cunningham (born 1911 in Cumberland, Maryland) spent his early life in Montana, studied at Stanford, and is now a professor of English at Brandeis University. An eminent scholar and critic, Cunningham has written *Tradition and Poetic Structure*, *The Renaissance in England*, and other studies. His poetry has tended toward great terseness and firm control; he is a master of the epigram. "Poetry is what looks like poetry, what sounds like poetry," he once defined. "It is metrical composition."

Collected Poems and Epigrams (1970).

James DenBoer (born 1937 in Sheboygan, Wisconsin) has worked as a writer and an editor for the United States Public Health Service and recently served as deputy director of special events for the White House Conference on Children and Youth. He is a graduate of Calvin College and of the University of California at Santa Barbara.

Learning the Way (1968), *Trying to Come Apart* (1971).

Emily Dickinson (1830–1886) passed nearly all her life as a semi-recluse at her family home in Amherst, Massachusetts. Her father was a prominent lawyer and (for a time) United States congressman. In her lifetime she published seven poems. The extent of her work was known only after her death, when her manuscripts were discovered in a trunk in the homestead attic. From 1890 until midcentury, nine post-humous collections of her poems were assembled by friends and relatives, some of whom rewrote her work to make it more conventional.

The Poems of Emily Dickinson, ed. Thomas H. Johnson, 3 vols. (1958), *The Complete Poems of Emily Dickinson,* in one vol., ed. Thomas H. Johnson (1960).

John Donne (1572–1631), English metaphysical poet and divine, wrote his subtle love lyrics as a young man and his "Holy Sonnets" and other religious poems in later life. In his early years Donne had to struggle for patronage and security. In 1615 he took orders in the Church of England and later, as Dean of St. Paul's Cathedral, became a preacher known for his eloquence. Little read in the nineteenth century, Donne's work has had much influence in our time.

The Poems of John Donne, ed. H. J. C. Grierson (1912).

Bob Dylan (born 1941 in Duluth, Minnesota), folk singer and song-writer, changed his name from Robert Zimmerman, allegedly out of admiration for Dylan Thomas. Self-taught on guitar, piano, autoharp, and harmonica, Dylan intently studied folk music and the songs of his idol, Woody Guthrie. His performances in Greenwich Village clubs in 1960 led to record albums and concert tours. Dylan created folk-rock practically single-handedly. In his later work, since a near-fatal motorcycle accident, he has gravitated toward country-and-western.

The Bob Dylan Song Book (undated), *Tarantula* (a novel with prose-poems, 1971). Record albums (all on Columbia label): *Blonde on Blonde,* C2S 841; *Highway 61 Revisited,* CS 9189; *Bringing It All Back Home,* CS 9128; *Another Side of Bob Dylan,* CS 8993; *The Times They Are A-changin',* CS 8905; *The Freewheelin' Bob Dylan,* CS 8786; *Bob Dylan,* CS 8579; *Bob Dylan's Greatest Hits,* KCS 9463; *Nashville Skyline,* KCS 9825; *John Wesley Harding,* CS 9604.

Richard Eberhart (born 1904 in Austin, Minnesota) has served as schoolmaster, professor, navy officer, business executive, tutor to the prince of Siam, and poetry consultant to the Library of Congress. There is a critical biography of Eberhart by Joel H. Roache, *Richard Eberhart: The Progress of an American Poet* (1971).

Collected Poems 1930–1960 (1960), *Collected Verse Plays* (1962), *The Quarry* (1964), *Selected Poems* (1965), *Shifts of Being* (1968), *Fields of Grace* (1972). Record album: *Richard Eberhart Reading His Poetry,* Caedmon, TC 1243.

T. S. Eliot (1888–1965) was born of a New England family that had moved to St. Louis. After study at Harvard, Eliot emigrated to London, became a bank clerk and (later) an influential editor. In 1927 he became a British citizen. Early poems such as "The Love Song of J. Alfred Prufrock" and *The Waste Land,* allusive and seemingly disconnected, helped work a revolution in English-language poetry. Eliot, however, spoke for tradition in his sense of the continuity of Western civilization and in his adherence to the Anglican church. *Four Quartets,* completed in 1943, was his last major work of poetry. In later years he devoted himself to writing verse plays for the London and New York stage. He received the Nobel Prize for Literature in 1948.

Old Possum's Book of Practical Cats (1939), *Complete Poems and Plays 1909–1950* (1952), *The Confidential Clerk* (play, 1954), *The Elder Statesman* (play, 1958), *Collected Poems 1909–1962* (1963), *Poems Written in Early Youth* (1967), *The Waste Land,* ed. Valerie Eliot and annotated by Ezra Pound (1971). Record albums: *T. S. Eliot Reading Poems and Choruses,* Caedmon, TC 1045; *T. S. Eliot Reading The Waste Land and Other Poems,* Caedmon, TC 1326.

George P. Elliott (born 1918 in Knightstown, Pennsylvania) was educated at Berkeley, where he later taught. He has also been on the faculties of St. Mary's College, Barnard, and Cornell. At present he teaches at Syracuse University. Elliott is known as poet, novelist (*Parktilden Village, David Knudsen, In the World, Muriel*), literary critic, and short-story writer (*Among the Dangs, An Hour of Last Things*).

Fever and Chills (1961), *From the Berkeley Hills* (1969).

Ralph Waldo Emerson (1803–1882) quit the Unitarian ministry to preach his personal doctrine of the Over-Soul in writings and lectures. Living in Concord, Massachusetts, Emerson exerted deep influence as the friend and mentor of the Transcendentalists, a group that included Henry David Thoreau and Margaret Fuller. In one of his addresses, "The American Scholar" (1837), Emerson called for a vigorous and independent life of the mind ("We have listened too long to the courtly muses of Europe"). He wrote ably about poetry and produced a few enduring poems.

Complete Works, ed. E. W. Emerson, 12 vols. (1903–1904).

John Engels (born 1931 in South Bend, Indiana) was graduated from Notre Dame and the University of Iowa. He also studied at University College in Dublin. Engels teaches now at St. Michael's College and lives in North Williston, Vermont, "three minutes from one of the best trout streams in New England."

The Homer Mitchell Place (1968).

Clayton Eshleman (born 1935 in Indianapolis, Indiana) writes: "I began to write when I was a student at Indiana University in 1958. Rather than give a brief autobiographical sketch I would prefer here to say something about 'A Very Old Woman,' which is one of the first *poems* (as opposed to verse) I ever wrote, summer 1959 when I lived in Chapala, Mexico, in a little hut that faced a steep hill on top of

which was a small graveyard &
shrine. Mexico was that opening-up
of a sensuousness I had denied,
having been brought up in the
midwest. Mexico, that fresh rush of
the stink of life, that heavy lilac,
that heavy lime & manure, enough
to corner me, make me feel outwards
& dig in to begin my own push."

Mexico & North (1961), *The
Chavin Illumination* (1965),
Lachrymae Mateo (1966), *Walks*
(1967), *Brother Stones* (1968), *Canta-
loups & Splendor* (1968), *T'ai* (1968),
The House of Okumura (1969),
Indiana (1969), *The Yellow River
Record* (1969), *The House of Ibuki*
(1969), *A Pitchblende* (1969), *Altars*
(1971), *Coils* (1972).

Dave Etter (born 1928 in Huntington
Park, California) was graduated in
1953 from the University of Iowa. He
has published his poems widely in
little magazines and anthologies.
With his wife and two children, he
lives now in Geneva, Illinois.

Go Read the River (1966), *The Last
Train to Prophetstown* (1968),
Strawberries (1970).

Donald Finkel (born 1929 in New
York City) went to Columbia
University and the University of
Iowa. His work has been recognized
with several awards and a Guggen-
heim fellowship. With his wife, the
poet Constance Urdang, and three
children, he lives in St. Louis, where
he teaches at Washington University.

The Clothing's New Emperor (in
Poets of Today VI, 1959), *Simeon*
(1964), *A Joyful Noise* (1966), *Answer
Back* (1968), *The Garbage Wars*
(1970), *Adequate Earth* (1972).

Calvin Forbes (born 1945 in Newark,
New Jersey) teaches at Emerson
College in Boston and is a contribu-
tor to *Poetry* and other magazines.
He has been working on a first
collection, to be called *Blue Monday*.

Robert Frost (1874–1963), although
born in San Francisco and first
recognized in England, came to be
popularly known as a spokesman of
rural Vermont. Between periods of
farming and schoolteaching, Frost
struggled hard until past forty to
support his family and to publish his
work. A recent biographer, Lawrance
Thompson, has recorded Frost's
private desperations. Audiences
responded warmly to his public
readings, and in late years Frost
became a sort of elder statesman and
poet laureate of the John F. Kennedy
administration, invited to read a
poem at President Kennedy's
inauguration and sent to Russia as
a cultural emissary. Frost early
mastered and excelled in the art of
laying conversational speech along a
metrical line.

The Poems of Robert Frost,
ed. Edward Connery Latham (1969).
Record album: *Robert Frost Reading*,
Caedmon, TC 1060.

Allen Ginsberg (born 1926 in
Newark, New Jersey) went to
Columbia College and served in the
merchant marine. His poem "Howl,"
read aloud to audiences in San
Francisco, helped establish the
celebrity of a Beat generation of
poets in the 1950's. Since then,
Ginsberg has been a prominent
spokesman for the counterculture,
campaigning for the legalization of

346

marijuana, attacking the CIA, regaling throngs on campuses with his poems and Hindu chants. Recently he issued a recording of the musical settings for the *Songs of Innocence and Experience* of William Blake.

Howl and Other Poems (1956), *Kaddish* (1960), *Empty Mirror: Early Poems* (1961), *Reality Sandwiches* (1963), *Wichita Vortex Sutra* (1966), *Planet News* (1968). Record album: *Allen Ginsberg Reads Howl and Other Poems*, Fantasy 7006.

Paul Goodman, (1911–1972), born in New York City, had a Renaissance-man breadth to his knowledge. His many books include works of psychology, urban planning, social criticism, fiction, drama, and poetry. He taught at many universities and in the New York and Cleveland institutes for Gestalt therapy. In *Growing Up Absurd* (1960), he showed himself a sympathetic critic of young people and an outspoken critic of bureaucracies.

The Lordly Hudson (1962), *Hawkweed* (1967), *Homespun of Oatmeal Gray* (1970).

Donald Hall (born 1928 in New Haven, Connecticut) went to Harvard and later Oxford, where he received the Newdigate Prize for poetry in 1952. One of the founding editors of *The Paris Review*, he has also compiled anthologies and has written a play (*An Evening's Frost*), critical books on Henry Moore and Marianne Moore, and a memoir, *String Too Short to Be Saved* (1961). He teaches at the University of Michigan.

The Alligator Bride: Poems New and Selected (1969), *The Yellow Room* (1971).

John Hartford (born 1937 in New York City) grew up in St. Louis, Missouri, where his father was a doctor. By age thirteen, Hartford had learned to play the fiddle and the five-string banjo. He worked as a disc jockey, a commercial artist, and a deck hand on the Mississippi, then settled in Nashville and began writing songs and performing them. His song "Gentle on My Mind" brought him national fame in 1967.

Word Movies (1971). Record albums: *Earthwords and Music*, RCA Victor LPM/LSP 3796; *Love Album*, RCA Victor LPM/LSP 3884.

Robert Hayden (born 1913 in Detroit) studied at the University of Michigan and Wayne State University before teaching for many years at Fisk University. He is now back at Michigan as professor of English. In 1965 his *Ballad of Remembrance* won first prize for poetry at the World Festival of Negro Arts in Dakar, Senegal.

Selected Poems (1966), *Words in the Mourning Time* (1969).

Anthony Hecht (born 1923 in New York City) went to Bard College and Columbia. He taught at Bard, Kenyon, Smith, and the University of Iowa and now teaches at the University of Rochester. In World War II he served with the army infantry in both Europe and the Pacific. He received the Pulitzer Prize for poetry in 1968.

A Summoning of Stones (1954), *The Hard Hours* (1967).

347

David Henderson (born 1942 in Harlem) has stayed in New York City, studying at Hunter College and the New School for Social Research, teaching at City College of New York. LeRoi Jones wrote an introduction to Henderson's first collection, and Henderson has since been editor of *Umbra*, a magazine devoted to black culture and poetry.

Felix of the Silent Planet (1967), *De Mayor of Harlem* (1970).

George Herbert (1593–1633), English devotional poet, the son of an aristocratic family, entered the priesthood of the Church of England and chose to live out his days in a country parish.

The Works of George Herbert, ed. F. E. Hutchinson (1941).

Robert Hershon (born 1935 in Brooklyn, New York), after living for a while in San Francisco, is back in Brooklyn, with his wife and two children, working as writer for a publisher of reference works and co-editing *Hanging Loose*, an unstapled poetry quarterly.

Swans Loving Bears Burning the Melting Deer (1967), *Atlantic Avenue* (1970), *4-Telling* (with Dick Lourie, Marge Piercy, and Emmett Jarrett, 1971), *Grocery Lists* (1971), *Little Red Wagon Painted Blue* (1972).

Daniel Hoffman (born 1923 in New York City) is known not only for his poetry but for his work as a scholar of folklore and as a literary critic. His study *Poe Poe Poe Poe Poe Poe Poe* appeared in 1972. He teaches at the University of Pennsylvania.

An Armada of Thirty Whales (1954), *A Little Geste* (1960), *The City of Satisfactions* (1963), *Striking the Stones* (1968), *Broken Laws* (1970).

A. D. Hope (born 1907 in Cooma, New South Wales) is the most eminent poet in Australia. He studied at Sydney and Oxford universities. For years Hope worked on his poetry but was forty-eight when he finally brought out his first collection. He has written significant criticism (*The Cave and the Spring* is a recent collection of essays on poetry) and is currently professor of English at Australian National University.

Collected Poems (1966), *New Poems: 1965–1969* (1970), *A Midsummer Eve's Dream: Variations on a Theme by William Dunbar* (1971).

Gerard Manley Hopkins (1844–1889) was born in Essex, England, and became a convert to Roman Catholicism. He spent his mature years as a Jesuit priest. In his lifetime, Hopkins' strange and original poems were known only to a few friends, among them Robert Bridges, who in 1918, long after the poet's death, published them. They have had a deep impact on recent poets, including Dylan Thomas.

Poems of Gerard Manley Hopkins, 4th ed., ed. W. H. Gardner and N. H. MacKenzie (1967).

A. E. Housman (1859–1936), English poet and scholar of Latin, published only two thin collections in his lifetime — the enormously popular *A Shropshire Lad* (1898) and the conclusively titled *Last Poems* (1922).

The Collected Poems of A. E. Housman (1959).

Ted Hughes (born 1930 in Mytholmroyd, Yorkshire, England) is one of the most influential contemporary poets in England. The son of a carpenter and tobacconist, Hughes worked at a variety of jobs — as Royal Air Force technician, chauffeur, gardener, night watchman, reader for a film studio. As a student at Cambridge University he met and married the poet Sylvia Plath. Besides poetry, Hughes has writen an acting version of Seneca's *Oedipus* and some beautiful and bizarre stories and verses for children.

The Hawk in the Rain (1957), *Lupercal* (1960), *Wodwo* (1967), *Crow* (1970).

Richard Hugo (born 1923 in Seattle, Washington) has informed his poems with many landscapes, in particular those of the Pacific Northwest. For a time he worked for an aircraft corporation; currently he is an English professor at the University of Montana.

A Run of Jacks (1961), *Death of the Kapowsin Tavern* (1965), *Good Luck in Cracked Italian* (1969).

David Ignatow (born 1914 in Brooklyn, New York) has captured in many of his poems the speech and cadences of city life. He has taught at several colleges, among them Columbia, Vassar, and Long Island University.

Poems 1934–1969 (1970).

Randall Jarrell (1914–1965) was born in Nashville, Tennessee, and served in World War II in the air force. His one novel, *Pictures from an Institution*, is a satire set on a campus (Jarrell was a teacher at the University of North Carolina at Greensboro). Famous also for *Poetry and the Age* and other literary criticism, Jarrell wrote many books for children and translations of poetry.

Complete Poems (1969). Record album: *Randall Jarrell Reads His Poetry*, Caedmon, TC 1363.

Robinson Jeffers (1887–1962) was born in Pittsburgh but lived most of his life in California. For a time he studied medicine, then devoted himself to poetry, living in Carmel by the Pacific in a stone house he built with his own hands. The vein of bitterness and misanthropy that runs through Jeffers' poems did not stop them from reaching a wide audience. He was one of few twentieth-century American poets to sustain long narrative and dramatic poems — *Roan Stallion*, *Tamar*, *Dear Judith*, *The Tower Beyond Tragedy*, and a version of the *Medea* of Euripides, performed in New York City with Judith Anderson.

Selected Poetry (1959), *The Beginning and the End* (1963).

Ben Jonson (1572?–1637), friend of Shakespeare and Donne, was a classicist by literary temperament, a brawler by disposition. Once jailed for helping to write a political satire, Jonson narrowly escaped another sentence after he dueled with, and slew, a fellow actor. His comedies (among them *Volpone* and *The Alchemist*) are among the crown jewels of the Elizabethan stage. His precise Latinate lyrics and epigrams inspired many imitations.

The Complete Poetry of Ben Jonson, ed. William B. Hunter, Jr. (1963).

John Keats (1795–1821), son of a London stable keeper, studied to become a physician, then decided on poetry as a career. Despite the hostility of critics to his early poem *Endymion*, Keats persisted, producing a deepening body of fine work, some of it reflecting his love for Fanny Brawne. Stricken with tuberculosis, Keats moved to Italy in hopes of regaining his health. He died in Rome and was there interred beneath the epitaph he wrote for himself: "Here lies one whose name was writ in water."

The Poetical Works of John Keats, ed. H. W. Garrod, 2nd ed. (1958).

B. B. King (born 1925 in Itta Bern, Mississippi), blues singer and composer, began as Riley B. King, disc jockey and singer on Memphis radio. After teaching himself guitar in 1945, he spent the next twenty years playing one-night stands along what he calls "the chitlin' circuit" in the South. Since the late 1960's his appearances and record albums have been winning a wider audience. Recently he has been giving free concerts to inmates of prisons. Both as songwriter and as performer, he is one of the living masters of the blues.

Record albums: *Blues on Top of Blues*, Blues Way, BLWS 6011; *His Best/The Electric B. B. King*, Blues Way, BLWS 6022; *Live and Well*, Blues Way, BLWS 6031; *B. B. King*

Sings Spirituals, Crown 5119; *My Kind of Blues*, Crown 5188; *Blues in My Heart*, Crown 5309; *Mr. Blues*, ABC S-456; *B. B. King Live at the Regal*, ABC S-509; *Confessin' the Blues*, ABC S-528; *Indianola, Mississippi*, ABC S-713; *B. B. King Live at Cook County Jail*, ABC S-723.

Galway Kinnell (born 1927 in Providence, Rhode Island) has lived in New York City, Vermont, Chicago, France, and Iran (this last the locale of his novel *Black Light*, 1966). He has translated books of poetry by François Villon and Yves Bonnefoy and from time to time has been a teacher and resident poet at several universities.

What a Kingdom It Was (1960), *Flower Herding on Mount Monadnock* (1964), *Body Rags* (1968), *The Book of Nightmares* (1971).

Carolyn Kizer (born 1925 in Spokane, Washington) has lived in China, Pakistan, Washington, D.C. (where she headed the literary program of the National Council on the Arts during the Johnson administration), and, at present, resides in Chapel Hill, North Carolina, where she is poet-in-residence at the University. "I am a premature Women's Liberationist," Miss Kizer has remarked. "I was writing poems on the subject ten years before it became fashionable, and a great many people, then, didn't understand what the hell the fuss was all about." For a time, she served as editor of the Seattle-based magazine *Poetry Northwest*.

Midnight Was My Cry: New and Selected Poems (1971).

John Knoepfle (born 1923 in Cincinnati), whose name is pronounced "No-ful," is a poet of many concerns. A folklore scholar and collector, he has recorded the voices of some seventy steamboatmen and is compiling a dialect study of speech along the inland rivers. Knoepfle has also translated the poems of Cesar Vallejo and Pablo Neruda (with Robert Bly and James Wright) and has published two books of verse for children. He is now director of the writing program and writer-in-residence at Saint Louis University.

Rivers into Islands (1965), *Songs for Gail Guidry's Guitar* (1969), *After Gray Days and Other Poems* (1969), *An Affair of Culture* (1969), *The Intricate Land* (1970), *The Ten-Fifteen Community Poems* (1971).

Bill Knott (born 1940 in Carson City, Michigan) signed his first poems with the name Saint Geraud (hero of an eighteenth-century French pornographic novel). In 1966 he circulated the report of his suicide, and since then his work has been signed "Bill Knott (1940–1966)."

The Naomi Poems: Corpse and Beans (signed Saint Geraud, 1968), *Aurealism: A Study* (1970), *Are You Ready Mary Baker Eddy* (with James Tate, 1970), *Nights of Naomi (Plus 2 Songs)* (1970), *Auto-necrophelia* (1971).

Maxine Kumin (born 1925 in Philadelphia) was graduated from Radcliffe and now lives in Newton, Massachusetts. Mrs. Kumin has written, in addition to her poetry, three novels and numerous books for children, some of them in collaboration with Anne Sexton.

Halfway (1961), *The Privilege* (1965), *The Nightmare Factory* (1970), *Up Country: Poems of New England* (1972).

Stanley Kunitz (born 1905 in Worcester, Massachusetts) is the editor of *Twentieth Century Authors* and other standard reference works of authors' biography. At present he edits the Yale Series of Younger Poets, helps direct the Work Center for the Fine Arts in Provincetown, and teaches at Columbia University. A meticulous poet, Kunitz has published a book about once every fourteen years. He was recognized with the Pulitzer Prize in 1958.

Selected Poems 1928–1958 (1958), *The Testing-Tree* (1971).

Greg Kuzma (born 1944 in Rome, New York) studied at Syracuse University and is currently teaching writing at the University of Nebraska. Proprietor of the Best Cellar Press, Kuzma publishes a pamphlet series and *Pebble*, a magazine of poetry.

Harry's Things (1971), *The Bosporus* (1971), *Song for Someone Going Away* (1971), *The Buffalo Hunt* (1972), *Good News* (1973).

Peter La Farge (1931–1965), American Indian singer and songwriter, was born in Fountain, Colorado, a member of the Nargaset tribe, and grew up in the Rocky Mountains. He was the adopted son of the novelist Oliver La Farge. From boyhood he worked as a cowhand, later competed in rodeos, served in the army in Korea, boxed twenty-four prizefights, then came to prominence for his singing at the Newport Folk Festival. Among his popular songs are "Ira Hayes," "Black Stallion," "Coyote," and "As Long as the Grass Shall Grow." He has influenced the young singer-songwriter Buffy Sainte-Marie, whose song "Now That the Buffalo's Gone" is dedicated to him.

Record albums: *As Long as the Grass Shall Grow*, Folkways 2532; *Peter La Farge Sings of the Cowboys*, Folkways 2533; *On the Warpath*, Folkways 2535.

Philip Larkin (born 1922 in Coventry, England), called the most influential British poet since World War II, went to Oxford. Since 1955 he has been librarian for the University of Hull at Yorkshire. Larkin has written novels (*Jill, A Girl in Winter*) and for years reviewed jazz records for a London newspaper. In his subtle and traditionally structured poems, the speaking voice of a tough-minded, disillusioned, self-deprecating protagonist facing a dreary urban landscape of quiet frustration and belt-tightening drew an immediate response from postwar English readers.

The Less Deceived (1955), *The Whitsun Weddings* (1964), *The North Ship* (1945, revised 1966).

Irving Layton (born 1912 near Bucharest, Rumania) is among the best known of living poets in Canada. As a child he settled with his parents in Montreal. During World War II he served as an officer in the Royal Canadian Artillery. Outspoken and controversial in his views, Layton is familiar to Canadian audiences because of his many public appearances, broadcasts, and telecasts. Recently he has been given high recognition — the Governor-General's Medal, two Canada Council awards, and other honors. At present he is a professor at York University in Toronto.

The Collected Poems of Irving Layton (1971).

Jay Leifer (born 1954 in Fargo, North Dakota) attended Cornell University "briefly to the point of satiety" and now lives on a communal farm in New Hampshire. He is currently working on "an astrological novel to be 5,000 pages long."

Denise Levertov (born 1923 in Ilford, Essex, England), daughter of a Jewish-born priest of the Anglican church, came to the United States in 1948. Her discovery of American poets, among them William Carlos Williams, apparently helped change the direction of her work, which had begun in formal conventions. With Robert Creeley and others of the Black Mountain group, she has exerted much influence among younger poets. She lives in Brookline, Massachusetts, with her husband Mitchell Goodman, a poet, novelist, and political activist.

Here and Now (1957), *Overland to the Islands* (1958), *With Eyes at the Back of Our Heads* (1959), *The Jacob's Ladder* (1961), *O Taste and See* (1964), *The Sorrow Dance* (1967), *Relearning the Alphabet* (1970), *To Stay Alive* (1971).

Philip Levine (born 1928 in Detroit) has been a factory worker, a truck driver, and a college teacher, most recently at Fresno State College in California.

On the Edge (1963), *Not This Pig* (1968), *Red Dust* (1971), *Pili's Wall* (1971), *They Feed They Lion* (1972).

Lou Lipsitz (born 1938 in Brooklyn, New York) has held jobs as a dishwasher, a reporter, and a garment worker. He studied at Chicago and Yale and now teaches political science at the University of North Carolina.

Cold Water (1967).

Robert Lowell (born 1917 in Boston) comes from a famous New England family. He attended Harvard, then was graduated from Kenyon College, where he studied with the poet and critic John Crowe Ransom. Lowell's early poems, violent in their imagery and tightly formal in their patterns, brought him a Pulitzer Prize in 1947. With *Life Studies*, in 1959, his work became more open in form, more colloquial in speech, and more direct in its use of his own experience. Lowell has actively served his political conscience. During World War II he spent time in a federal prison for resisting the draft. More recently (detailed in his *Notebook*) he has been involved in protest against the Vietnam war. He has written significant plays (*The Old Glory*), as well as English versions of the *Phaedra* of Racine and the *Prometheus Bound* of Aeschylus.

Land of Unlikeness (1944), *Lord Weary's Castle* (1946), *The Mills of the Kavanaughs* (1951), *Life Studies* (1959), *Imitations* (1961), *For the Union Dead* (1964), *Near the Ocean* (1967), *Notebook* (1969, revised 1970).

Roger McGough (born 1937 in Liverpool, England) has written, "I was born in a working-class home where, if you're a poet, it's something to be ashamed of." One of an active group of Liverpool popular poets, McGough has read aloud in pubs and in the open air and has written plays, satirical sketches, and a "mini-novel," *Frinck*.

Watchwords (1969), *Penguin Modern Poets 10: The Mersey Sound* (with Adrian Henri and Brian Patten, 1967).

Archibald MacLeish (born 1892 in Glencoe, Illinois) has been both poet and public servant. From 1939 to 1944 he served as Librarian of Congress and during World War II was an assistant secretary of state. In 1945, he was chief of the American delegation to draw up a constitution for UNESCO. Since then, he has taught at Harvard and Amherst and has written two Broadway-produced plays (*J.B.* in 1958 and *Scratch* in 1971, the latter based on Stephen Vincent Benét's story "The Devil and Daniel Webster").

Collected Poems 1917–1952 (1963), *Songs for Eve* (1954), *"The Wild Old Wicked Man" and Other Poems* (1968), *The Human Season: Selected Poems 1926–1972* (1972). Record album: *Archibald MacLeish Reads His Poetry*, Caedmon, TC 1009.

Andrew Marvell (1621–1678), English poet and statesman, was for a while Oliver Cromwell's Latin secretary (together with Milton). At the time of his death he was a member of Parliament.

Poems and Letters of Andrew Marvell, ed. H. M. Margoliouth, 2nd ed. (1952).

William Meredith (born 1919 in New York City) went to Princeton and served during World War II as a navy aviator. Once a copy boy and cub reporter for *The New York Times*, he has taught at Princeton, the Bread Loaf Writers Conference, the University of Hawaii, and (since 1955) Connecticut College. He has translated *Alcools* (poems of Guillaume Apollinaire) and has edited the poems of Shelley. He is a chancellor of the Academy of American Poets and a member of the National Institute of Arts and Letters.

Earth Walk: New and Selected Poems (1970).

James Merrill (born 1926 in New York City) was graduated from Amherst College. Besides his poetry, which received the National Book Award in 1966, Merrill has written novels, *The Seraglio* and *The (Diblos) Notebook*, and two plays produced off-Broadway. He lives in Stonington, Connecticut.

First Poems (1951), *The Country of a Thousand Years of Peace* (1959, revised 1970), *Water Street* (1962), *Nights and Days* (1966), *The Fire Screen* (1969), *Braving the Elements* (1972).

W. S. Merwin (born 1927 in New York City) grew up in Union City, New Jersey, and Scranton, Pennsylvania. After graduation from Princeton, he worked as a tutor in France, Portugal, and Majorca. Merwin has been prolific as a translator (*The Poem of the Cid, Spanish Ballads, The Satires of Perseus, The Song of Roland, Selected Translations 1948–1968*). He has written plays, articles, radio scripts, and a book of prose, *The Miner's Pale Children*. In 1971 he received the Pulitzer Prize for poetry.

A Mask for Janus (1952), *The Dancing Bears* (1954), *Green with Beasts* (1956), *The Drunk in the Furnace* (1960), *The Moving Target* (1963), *The Lice* (1967), *The Carrier of Ladders* (1970). Record album: *W. S. Merwin Reading His Poetry*, Caedmon, TC 1295.

Bert Meyers (born 1929 in Los Angeles) worked for ten years as a picture-framer, then was accepted as a candidate for a master's degree at Claremont Graduate School, even though he had never attended college. He now teaches English at Pitzer College in Claremont, California, where he lives with his wife and two children. His poetry has received two Ingram-Merrill awards and a grant from the National Endowment for the Arts.

Early Rain (1960), *The Dark Birds* (1968).

John Milton (1608–1674), English poet and pamphlet writer, laid plans as a young man to compose a poem of epic dimensions. It was delayed by his duties in support of the Puritan cause — writing tracts and later serving as Oliver Cromwell's secretary. Driven into retirement at the Restoration, brought to complete blindness from paperwork, Milton at last composed his major heroic poem *Paradise Lost* (1667), followed by *Paradise Regained* (1671) and his tragedy *Samson Agonistes* (1671).

The Complete English Poetry of John Milton, ed. John T. Shawcross (revised 1971).

Richard Moore (born 1927 in Greenwich, Connecticut) served as a pilot in the air force and is now teaching at the New England Conservatory of Music.

A Question of Survival (1971), *Word from the Hills* (1972).

Howard Moss (born 1922 in New York City) has long been poetry editor of *The New Yorker*. He is the author of a play, *The Folding Green;* a study of Marcel Proust; and *Writing Against Time*, a book of criticism. In 1972 he received the National Book Award for poetry.

A Winter Come, a Summer Gone: Poems 1946–1960 (1960), *Finding Them Lost and Other Poems* (1965), *Second Nature* (1968), *Selected Poems* (1971).

Geoffrey Movius (born 1940 in Boston) wrote a Harvard dissertation on the work of William Carlos Williams and is now at Tufts University, where he teaches modern poetry. A contributor to *Boston Review*, *Harvard Advocate*, and the anthology *Peace Feelers*, he lives in Cambridge, Massachusetts, with his wife and two children.

Howard Nemerov (born 1920 in New York City) was graduated from Harvard in 1941 and served in World War II as a fighter pilot. As well as for poetry, Nemerov is known for his novels — *The Melodramatists, Federigo, or The Power of Love, The Homecoming Game* — and his short stories in *A Commodity of Dreams* and *Stories, Fables & Other Diversions*. He has taught at Hamilton and Bennington colleges and Brandeis University and now teaches at Washington University in St. Louis.

New and Selected Poems (1960), *The Next Room of the Dream* (1962), *The Blue Swallows* (1967).

John Frederick Nims (born 1913 in Muskegon, Michigan) has taught at Notre Dame, Toronto, Illinois, and Harvard universities and has held visiting professorships in Florence, Madrid, and Milan. He is now a professor at the University of Illinois at Chicago. A distinguished translator of poetry from languages as varied as classical Greek, Catalan, and Galician, Nims has made translations into English of *The Poems of St. John of the Cross*, Euripides' *Andromache*, and recently a large anthology, *Sappho to Valéry*.

The Iron Pastoral (1947), *A Fountain in Kentucky* (1950), *Knowledge of the Evening* (1960), *Of Flesh and Bone* (1967).

Bink Noll (born 1927 in South Orange, New Jersey) went to Princeton, Johns Hopkins, and the University of Colorado, and served for two years in the merchant marine. He taught at Dartmouth, held a Fulbright grant to teach in Spain, and now teaches at Beloit College in Wisconsin.

The Center of the Circle (1962), *The Feast* (1967).

355

Gregory Orr (born 1947 in Albany, New York) grew up in the rural Hudson River Valley and went to Hamilton and Antioch colleges. He has studied on a scholarship in the writing program at Columbia University and won an award from the New York City Poetry Center. Orr has supported himself by working in a New York bookstore. He is a member of the Society of Fellows at the University of Michigan.

Robert Pack (born 1929 in New York City) now is poet-in-residence at Middlebury College in Vermont. He has published children's literature, translations of the librettos of Mozart's operas, anthologies, and a critical study of the poetry of Wallace Stevens.

Selected Poems (1964), *Home from the Cemetery* (1969), *Nothing but Light* (1973).

Patrice Phillips (born 1949 in Bucks County, Pennsylvania) was graduated from Jackson College in 1971. Besides working for the catering establishment depicted in her poem "The Function Room," she has served as a dance therapist at Metropolitan State Hospital in Waltham, Massachusetts.

Marge Piercy (born 1934 in Detroit) has lived in Chicago, Boston, San Francisco, New York City, and Cape Cod. She helped found the Brooklyn chapter of Students for a Democratic Society. Besides poetry, she has written two novels—*Going Down Fast* and *Dance the Eagle to Sleep*.

Breaking Camp (1968), *Hard Loving* (1969), *4-Telling* (with Robert Hershon, Emmett Jarrett, and Dick Lourie, 1971), *The Crossing* (1971).

Sylvia Plath (1932–1963) was born in Boston, the daughter of an expert on bees, and was graduated from Smith College and Cambridge University. Like Esther Greenwood, the protagonist in her one novel, *The Bell Jar* (first published under a pen name in 1963), Sylvia Plath won a student contest that sent her to work in New York for a national magazine and struggled against mental illness. In 1956 she married the English poet Ted Hughes and settled permanently in England. She died by her own hand, leaving two children. Her posthumous collection *Ariel* has been acclaimed.

The Colossus (1962), *Ariel* (1966), *Crossing the Water* (1971), *Winter Trees* (1972).

Edgar Allan Poe (1809–1849), adopted son of a wealthy Virginia merchant, dropped out of West Point and entered a hard grind of hack writing and magazine editing to support himself and his sickly child-bride. Poe's tales of ethereal beauties, tormented heroes, Gothic houses, and bizarre landscapes have lasted well, as have a few of his poems. Alcoholism and the death of his wife aggravated his quarrels with himself, and he was found dying in the streets of Baltimore, apparently having been plied with drinks and voted by ballot-box stuffers.

Collected Works, Vol. 1, Poems, ed. T. O. Mabbott (1969).

David Ray (born 1932 in Sapulpa, Oklahoma) holds two degrees from the University of Chicago. With Robert Bly, he founded the organization American Writers Against the Vietnam War. He has edited two political poetry anthologies, *From the Hungarian Revolution* and (with Bly) *A Poetry Reading Against the Vietnam War*. He has taught at Cornell, Reed, and Northern Illinois and is currently teaching at the University of Missouri at Kansas City, where he edits the magazine *New Letters*.

X-Rays (1965), *Dragging the Main* (1968).

Thomas Dillon Redshaw (born 1944 in Salem, Massachusetts) is a graduate of Tufts University. He has studied at University and Trinity colleges in Dublin and at New York University. In Ireland, he published pamphlets of his poems and edited collections by the Irish poets Lyle Donaghy and Thomas MacGreevy. At present he is teaching at the College of St. Thomas in Minnesota.

Tim Reynolds (born 1936 in Vicksburg, Mississippi) has lived in Mexico, Japan, and Europe. For a time he taught Latin and Greek in high school and later in the University of Texas. His play *Peace*, an adaptation from Aristophanes, had an off-Broadway run in 1969.

Ryoanji (1964), *Halflife* (1964), *Catfish Goodbye* (1967), *Slocum* (1968), *Que* (1971).

Adrienne Rich (born 1929 in Baltimore) published her first book of poems while still a Radcliffe undergraduate. Later she studied at

Oxford, lived for a time in Holland, and more recently has been teaching in the City College of New York.

A Change of World (1951), *The Diamond Cutters* (1955), *Snapshots of a Daughter-in-Law* (1963), *Necessities of Life* (1966), *Leaflets* (1969), *The Will to Change* (1971).

John Ridland (born 1933 in England) grew up in southern California and went to Swarthmore College, Berkeley, and Claremont Graduate School. Editor and publisher for several years of the poetry magazine *Little Square Review*, he is currently teaching at the University of California at Santa Barbara. His "Assassination Poems" apparently date from 1968, the year of the slayings of Martin Luther King and Robert Kennedy.

Fires of Home (1961), *Ode on Violence and Other Poems* (1969).

Martin Robbins (born 1931 in Denver, Colorado) is a poet, playwright, translator, and baritone who has appeared widely as a soloist. He has been teaching English at Northeastern University for the past nine years.

A Refrain of Roses (1965), *A Reply to the Headlines* (1970).

Edwin Arlington Robinson (1869–1935) was born in Head Tide, Maine, and attended Harvard until his family ran out of money. Fond of portraying failures, reprobates, and heavy drinkers (the characters with whom he populated his semi-fictitious Tilbury Town), Robinson viewed life with stoic pessimism. He struggled through a series of ill-paying odd jobs until befriended by President Theodore Roosevelt, who liked his poetry. *Tristram* (1927), an Arthurian narrative poem, was a best-seller. Robinson brought hard-eyed realism to his New England landscapes and combined tight stanzas with colloquial language long before Robert Frost.

Collected Poems (1949).

Theodore Roethke (1908–1963) was born in Saginaw, Michigan, where his family ran a large greenhouse. (No poet's work is wealthier in its knowledge of vegetation.) Roethke's poetry developed from rather conventional and imitative lyrics through a phase of wildly disconnected stream-of-consciousness into (at the end) a meditative poetry reminiscent in its open lines of Walt Whitman's. For many years Roethke was an influential teacher at the University of Washington. *The Glass House: The Life of Theodore Roethke* (1968), by Allan Seager, is a biography.

Collected Poems (1966), *Straw for the Fire: From the Notebooks of Theodore Roethke 1943–1963*, ed. David Wagoner (1972). Record album: *Theodore Roethke Reads His Poetry*, Caedmon, TC 1351.

Gibbons Ruark (born 1941 in Raleigh, North Carolina) has taught at the University of North Carolina at Greensboro, where (with Robert Watson) he co-edited an anthology, *The Greensboro Reader*. His first book won an award from the National Council on the Arts. He is currently an English professor at the University of Delaware.

A Program for Survival (1970).

Raphael Rudnik (born 1933 in New York City) is a graduate of Bard and Columbia. For a time he worked as a writer of publicity for a philanthropic organization. Recently he has been living in Amsterdam.

A Lesson from the Cyclops (1969), *In the Heart and Our City* (1973).

Norman H. Russell (born 1921 in Big Stone Gap, Virginia), part Cherokee Indian, is a poet with an interest in collecting and transcribing American Indian folk materials. The author of seven textbooks in the sciences, he teaches biology at Buena Vista College in Storm Lake, Iowa.

indian thoughts (1972).

Dennis Saleh (born 1942 in Chicago) grew up in Fresno, California, where he went to college. Saleh studied for a time to be a psychologist, then switched to the graduate writing program at the University of California at Irvine. Later he taught at the same university in Riverside and in Santa Cruz. He is married, with one son. Recently, with James McMichael, he co-edited *Just What the Country Needs, Another Poetry Anthology*.

A Guide to Familiar American Incest (1971).

Stephen Sandy (born 1934 in Minneapolis, Minnesota) served in both the army and the navy. He was graduated from Yale and Harvard and has taught at Harvard, Brown, and Bennington. Sandy has also lived in Ireland and Japan.

Stresses in the Peaceable Kingdom
(1967), *Roofs* (1971).

Aram Saroyan (born 1943 in New York City), son of the writer William Saroyan, left Columbia College in his freshman year to wander Europe and America. One of the best-known figures in the Concrete Poetry movement, Saroyan has announced that he is not writing any more.

Works (1966), *Aram Saroyan* (1968), *Pages* (1969), *Words and Photographs* (1970).

James Schuyler (born 1923 in Chicago) has worked in New York City for *Art News* and for the Museum of Modern Art. Besides several plays produced off-Broadway, he has written a novel, *Alfred and Guinevere* (1958), and has collaborated with John Ashbery on another novel, *A Nest of Ninnies* (1969).

May 24th or So (1966), *Freely Espousing* (1969), *The Crystal Lithium* (1972).

Anne Sexton (born 1928 in Newton, Massachusetts) avoided college and once worked as a fashion model. Her first book, *To Bedlam and Partway Back*, with its frank evocations of mental illness, helped begin a season of "confessional poetry" in America. Mrs. Sexton has written a play produced in New York City and (with Maxine Kumin) books for children. With a group of musicians, she has recently been performing her poems under the collective name Anne Sexton and Her Kind. She received the Pulitzer Prize for poetry in 1966 and now lives in a suburb of Boston with her husband and two daughters.

To Bedlam and Partway Back (1960), *All My Pretty Ones* (1962), *Live or Die* (1966), *Love Poems* 1969), *Transformations* (1971), *The Book of Folly* (1972).

William Shakespeare (1565–1616) was born in Stratford-on-Avon and made his living as an actor and playwright in London. Earlier (it is said) he was a poacher of deer.

The Complete Signet Classic Shakespeare, ed. Sylvan Barnet and others (1972).

Harvey Shapiro (born 1924 in Chicago) finished his schooling at Yale and Columbia after serving as an air force radio gunner in World War II. He has worked on the staffs of *Commentary* and *The New Yorker* and, since 1957, has been a writer and editor for *The New York Times.*

The Eye (1953), *The Book and Other Poems* (1955), *Mountain, Fire, Thornbush* (1961), *Battle Report* (1966), *This World* (1971).

Percy Bysshe Shelley (1792–1822), English poet, was a lifelong rebel against convention. Ousted from Oxford for writing a tract, "The Necessity of Atheism," Shelley espoused both the radical social philosophy of William Godwin and later Godwin's daughter Mary (author of *Frankenstein*). The vigorous social protest of Shelley's poetry is tempered, perhaps diluted, by the intangible Neoplatonic idealism of his thought. *Prometheus Unbound* (1820), a drama, is to be reckoned with.

Works, ed. T. Hutchinson (1934).

Sir Philip Sidney (1554–1586), poet, member of Parliament, soldier, diplomat, and brilliant courtier in the era of Queen Elizabeth, wrote a major sequence of sonnets, *Astrophel and Stella;* a prose romance, *Arcadia;* and a *Defence of Poesy.* He died in battle in the Netherlands.

The Complete Works of Sir Philip Sidney, ed. A. Feuillerat (1912–1923).

Charles Simic (born 1938 in Chicago) was graduated from New York University, then worked for *Aperture,* a photography magazine. Recently he has been teaching at Hayward State College in California.

What the Grass Says (1967), *Somewhere Among Us a Stone Is Taking Notes* (1970), *Dismantling the Silence* (1971), *White* (1972).

Nina Simone (born 1933 in Tryon, North Carolina), singer, pianist, and composer, studied at Juilliard and Curtis Institute of Music. Since 1954 she has appeared in many nightclubs and concerts. Besides "Four Women," her original songs include "Mississippi Goddam" and "Backlash Blues" (this last with words by Langston Hughes).

Record albums: *Nina Simone in Concert,* Philips, PHS 600–135; *Wild Is the Wind,* Philips, PHS 600–207; *Silk & Soul,* RCA Victor, LSP 3837; *Nina Simone Sings the Blues,* RCA Victor, LSP 3789; *'Nuff Said,* RCA Victor, LSP 4065; *Black Gold,* RCA Victor, LSP 4248; *To Love Somebody,* RCA Victor, LSP 4152; *The Best of Nina Simone,* RCA Victor, LSP 4374.

Louis Simpson (born 1923 in Jamaica, British West Indies) came to this country in 1940 and took a Ph.D. from Columbia. The author of a novel, *Riverside Drive,* he worked for a time in publishing and now teaches at the State University of New York at Stony Brook. In 1964 he received the Pulitzer Prize for poetry.

At the End of the Open Road (1963), *Selected Poems* (1965), *Adventures of the Letter I* (1971).

L. E. Sissman (born 1928 in Detroit) has successively been a National Spelling Bee champion, a panelist on the old radio program "The Quiz Kids," a Harvard student expelled for "insubordination," an honors graduate of Harvard, a Fuller Brush man, a campaign aide to John F. Kennedy, a copy editor, and an executive in a Boston advertising firm.

Dying: An Introduction (1967), *Scattered Returns* (1969), *Pursuit of Honor* (1971).

Knute Skinner (born 1929 in St. Louis) studied at Colorado State College and the University of Iowa. In recent years, he has divided his time between teaching at Western Washington State College and living, with his wife and two sons, in a small cottage near Liscannon Bay, Ireland.

Stranger with a Watch (1965), *A Close Sky over Killaspuglonane* (1968), *In Dinosaur Country* (1969), *The Sorcerers* (1972).

William Jay Smith (born 1918 in Winnfield, Louisiana) has been a

Rhodes scholar at Oxford, a navy liaison officer on a French ship in World War II, a member of the Vermont state legislature, and Consultant in Poetry for the Library of Congress. At present, he is a professor at Hollins College in Virginia.

New & Selected Poems (1970).

W. D. Snodgrass (born 1926 in Wilkinsburg, Pennsylvania) was educated at Geneva College and at the State University of Iowa. He has taught English at Cornell, Rochester, Wayne State, and now teaches at Syracuse University. An accomplished amateur musician, Snodgrass has translated early German lyrics and (with Lore Segal) the *Gallows Songs* of Christian Morgenstern. In 1960 he received the Pulitzer Prize for poetry.

Heart's Needle (1959), *After Experience* (1968).

Gary Snyder (born 1930 in San Francisco) has spent most of his life on the West Coast and in Japan, with seasons as a student at Reed College and at Berkeley and as a logger, forest ranger, carpenter, seaman, college teacher, and member of a Zen community in Kyoto. *Earth House Hold* (1969) is a volume of journals and essays. In his poetry, Snyder questions the durability of Western civilization and anticipates a return to unity with the natural and primitive world.

Riprap (1959), *Myths and Texts* (1960), *Six Sections from Mountains and Rivers Without End* (1965), *A Range of Poems* (collected poems, published in England, 1966), *The*

Back Country (1968), *Regarding Wave* (1970).

Barry Spacks (born 1931 in Philadelphia) was graduated from the University of Pennsylvania and Indiana University. After army service he went to England as a Fulbright fellow. The author of two novels, *The Sophomore* and *Orphans*, he lives in Wellesley, Massachusetts, with his wife the scholar-critic Patricia Meyer Spacks and daughter. He teaches writing and literature at M.I.T.

The Company of Children (1969), *Something Human* (1972).

Skip (Alexander) Spence (born 1938 in Illinois) came to fame as drummer for the rock group The Moby Grape, then in 1969 branched out on his own.

Record album: *Oar*.

William Stafford (born 1914 in Hutchinson, Kansas) was interned as a conscientious objector during World War II. In many of his poems he embodies landscapes of the Midwest and of the Pacific Northwest, where he now lives, teaching at Lewis and Clark College in Oregon. Recently he served as Consultant in Poetry for the Library of Congress.

West of Your City (1960), *Traveling Through the Dark* (1962), *The Rescued Year* (1966), *Allegiances* (1970).

George Starbuck (born 1931 in Columbus, Ohio) studied at California Institute of Technology, Berkeley, Chicago, and Harvard. In 1960, he won the Yale Series of

Younger Poets Award for his first collection. He has worked as an editor for a Boston book publisher and has been director of creative writing programs at the University of Iowa and (currently) at Boston University.

Bone Thoughts (1960), *White Paper* (1966).

Wallace Stevens (1879–1955) was born in Reading, Pennsylvania, attended Harvard, practiced law in New York City, then went to work for an insurance company, of which he became vice-president. Once asked how he was able to combine poetry and insurance, Stevens replied that the two occupations had something in common — "calculated risk." Living quietly in Hartford, Connecticut, Stevens sought to discover order in the world by the operation of his subtle and exotic imagination. His critical essays, collected in *The Necessary Angel*, and his *Selected Letters*, edited by his daughter Holly Stevens, are central documents in the history of modern poetry.

Collected Poems (1954), *Opus Posthumous*, ed. Samuel French Morse (1957). Record album: *Wallace Stevens Reading His Poems*, Caedmon, TC 1068.

Mark Strand (born 1934 in Summerside, Prince Edward Island, Canada) was graduated from Antioch and Yale and lived for a while in Italy and in Brazil. At present he makes his home in New York City.

Sleeping with One Eye Open (1964), *Reasons for Moving* (1968), *Darker* (1970).

Marcia Stubbs (born 1928 in Newark, New Jersey) studied at the University of Michigan and at Stanford University and taught at Tufts University. At present, she is teaching at Wellesley College. A contributor to several little magazines, she lives with her husband and daughters in Lexington, Massachusetts.

May Swenson (born 1919 in Logan, Utah) worked as a reporter in Salt Lake City before moving to New York City. Her work has brought her a Shelley Memorial Award, the Brandeis University Arts Award, Guggenheim, Ford, and Rockefeller foundation fellowships, and an award from the National Institute of Arts and Letters. Some of her poems exhibit (in addition to their satisfactions as perfections of language) graphic shapes and visual elements. She makes her home at present in Sea Cliff, New York.

To Mix with Time: New and Selected Poems (1963), *Poems to Solve* (1966), *Half Sun, Half Sleep* (1967), *Iconographs* (1970).

Jonathan Swift (1667–1745), Anglo-Irish satirist, journalist, and clergyman, is best remembered for *Gulliver's Travels*, an affectionate tribute to the reasonable part of "that animal called man" and a scathing rebuke to the rest of him. In a life crowded with politics, literary society, platonic love-affairs, and finally the deanship of St. Patrick's Cathedral in Dublin, Swift found occasions for writing much verse.

Poetical Works, ed. Herbert Davis (1967).

James Tate (born 1943 in Kansas City, Missouri) studied and taught at the poetry workshop of the University of Iowa and has also taught at Berkeley, Columbia, Emerson College, and the University of Massachusetts. In 1966 he won the book competition of the Yale Series of Younger Poets.

The Lost Pilot (1967), *The Oblivion Ha-Ha* (1970), *Absences* (1972).

Henry Taylor (born 1942 in Virginia) was graduated from the University of Virginia and Hollins College and has taught at the University of Utah. Currently he is at American University in Washington, D.C.

The Horse Show at Midnight (1966), *Breakings* (1971).

Dylan Thomas (1914–1953) was born in Swansea, Wales, a town affectionately imaged in his *Under Milk Wood,* a play for voices. Much of Thomas' life was a bitter struggle to support his wife and family. Lacking a university education, he found most paying literary labor barred to him in England, although, a resonant reader-aloud of poetry, he made broadcasts for British radio and made popular reading tours of America. He died in a hospital in New York City.

The Poems of Dylan Thomas, ed. Daniel Jones (1971), *Under Milk Wood* (1954). Record album: *Dylan Thomas Reading His Complete Recorded Poetry,* Caedmon, TC 2014.

John Thompson (born 1918 in Grand Rapids, Michigan) has written a scholarly study, *The Founding of English Metre,* and has contributed reviews and essays to *Commentary* and *The New York Review of Books.* Former executive director of the Farfield Foundation, a philanthropy, he has traveled extensively in Europe, Asia, Africa, and Latin America. He now teaches English at the State University of New York at Stony Brook.

The Talking Girl and Other Poems (1968).

Anthony Thwaite (born 1930 in Chester, England), poet and critic, has taught at Tokyo University and the University of Libya. He has been a radio producer for the BBC and literary editor of two leading English magazines, *The Listener* and the *New Statesman.* He co-edited *The Penguin Book of Japanese Verse.*

Home Truths (1962), *The Owl in the Tree* (1963), *The Stones of Emptiness* (1967), *Penguin Modern Poets 18* (with A. Alvarez and Roy Fuller, 1970).

Walasse Ting (born 1939 in New York City) is a painter as well as a poet. He lives in New York, where he has attempted to bring the traditions of classical Chinese poetry to bear upon urban life.

Hot and Sour Soup (1970).

Constance Urdang (born 1922 in New York City) is a graduate of Smith College and the University of Iowa. She has written fiction as well as poetry and has edited a dictionary of famous people. Her husband is the poet Donald Finkel, her home is in St. Louis.

Charades and Celebrations (1965).

David Wagoner (born 1926 in Masillon, Ohio) has both studied and taught at the University of Washington, where he is now professor of English and editor of the magazine *Poetry Northwest.* Known for his fiction as well as for his poetry, Wagoner has published five novels, most recently, *Baby, Come on Inside.*

New and Selected Poems (1969), *Riverbed* (1972).

Diane Wakoski (born 1937 in Whittier, California) went to Berkeley and now lives in New York City. She has taught at the Bread Loaf Writers Conference. A prolific poet, she is especially popular as a reader of her work to young audiences.

Coins and Coffins (1962), *Discrepancies and Apparitions* (1966), *The George Washington Poems* (1967), *Inside the Blood Factory* (1968), *Greed, Parts 1 and 2* (1968), *Greed, Parts 3 and 4* (1969), *The Magellanic Clouds* (1970), *The Motorcycle Betrayal Poems* (1971), *Smudging* (1972).

Keith Waldrop (born 1932 in Emporia, Kansas) took his doctorate at the University of Michigan with a thesis on obscenity in literature. He has since taught at Wesleyan University and is now at Brown. Waldrop has acted in films and directed plays. Wherever he has lived he has engineered remarkable hoaxes that have deceived and entertained throngs. Translator of Ferdinand Alquié's *Philosophy of Surrealism,* he has received an Amy Lowell traveling fellowship and a nomination for the National Book Award for his own poems. He now lives in Providence, Rhode Island, with his wife the poet Rosmarie Waldrop, thousands of books, and a basement printing press that produces more books under the imprint Burning Deck.

A Windmill Near Calvary (1968), *To the Sincere Reader* (with art by Nelson Howe, 1969), *The Antichrist and Other Foundlings* (1970), *Songs from the Decline of the West* (1971), *My Nodebook for December* (1971).

Rosmarie Waldrop (born 1935 in Kitzingen, Germany) has studied in Germany and France and at the University of Michigan. She has taught at Wesleyan University. With Keith Waldrop, she edits, publishes, and sometimes prints Burning Deck books. Recently she completed a translation of Edmond Jabès' *The Book of Questions.*

A Dark Octave (1967), *Camp Printing* (1970), *The Relaxed Abalone* (1970), *Spring Is a Season and Nothing Else* (1971), *The Aggressive Ways of the Casual Stranger* (1972).

Robert Watson (born 1925 in Passaic, New Jersey) studied and taught at Williams and Johns Hopkins. He was a Swiss-American exchange fellow at the University of Zurich and is now professor of English at the University of North Carolina at Greensboro. He has written a novel, *Three Sides of the*

Mirror. The painter Elizabeth Rean is his wife.

A Paper Horse (1962), *Advantages of Dark* (1966), *Christmas in Las Vegas* (1971).

James Welch (born 1940 on an Indian reservation in Browning, Montana) is a Blackfoot Indian whose poems have attracted wide notice. He received the degree of master of fine arts from the University of Montana.

Riding the Earthboy 40 (1971).

Ruth Whitman (born 1922 in New York City) studied at Radcliffe and Harvard. She has been editor of the poetry magazine *Audience,* translator of the poetry of Jacob Glatstein, Alain Bosquet, several modern Greek poets, and translator-editor of *An Anthology of Modern Yiddish Poetry.* Recipient of the Reynolds Lyric Award, Jennie Tane Award, and Alice Fay Di Castagnola Award, she now teaches at Radcliffe and is director of the Poetry Writing Program in the Schools in Massachusetts under the Massachusetts Council and the National Endowment for the Arts. '

Blood & Milk Poems (1963), *The Marriage Wig* (1968), *The Passion of Lizzie Borden: New and Selected Poems* (1972).

Walt Whitman (1819–1892) was born on Long Island and spent his early years as a schoolteacher, a temperance propagandist, a printer, and a newspaper editor on the Brooklyn *Eagle.* His self-published *Leaves of Grass* (1855, later revised and enlarged continually) won praise

from Ralph Waldo Emerson and gained Whitman readers in England. Americans at first were slow to accept Whitman's unconventionally open verse forms, his sexual frankness, and his gregarious egoism. The poet of boundless faith in American democracy, Whitman's vision was tempered by his experiences as a volunteer hospital nurse during the Civil War (described in his poems *Drum Taps* and his wartime letters). In old age he saw his work finally winning acceptance. His impact on later American poetry has been profound.

Leaves of Grass: Comprehensive Reader's Edition, ed. Gay Wilson Allen, Sculley Bradley, and others (1965).

Dallas E. Wiebe (born 1930 in Newton, Kansas) has taught English at the universities of Michigan, Wisconsin, and Cincinnati. He is the author of a novel, *Skyblue the Badass* (1970). His work has appeared in *The Paris Review, Midwest, Burning Deck, Prairie Schooner, Counter/Measures,* and other magazines and in two cooperative anthologies.

The Wolgamot Interstice, ed. D. C. Hope (1961), *In the Late, Gnat Light,* ed. Dallas E. Wiebe (1965).

Richard Wilbur (born 1917 in New York City) was graduated from Amherst College and has taught English at Harvard and Wellesley. Currently, he is at Wesleyan University. In addition to writing poetry, for which he has received the Pulitzer Prize and the National Book Award, Wilbur has edited the poetry of Shakespeare and Poe, collaborated with Lillian Hellman on lyrics for a comic opera *Candide,* written *Loudmouse,* a story for children, and deftly translated three plays of Molière into English verse.

The Poems of Richard Wilbur (1963), *Walking to Sleep* (1969). Record album: *Richard Wilbur Reading His Poetry,* Caedmon, TC 1248.

Peter Wild (born 1940 in Easthampton, Massachusetts) has published widely in magazines and anthologies. For the past few years he has been living in the Southwest and is now on the creative writing faculty of the University of Arizona.

The Afternoon in Dismay (1968), *Mica Mtn Poems* (1968), *Sonnets* (1968), *Love Poems* (1969), *Fat Man Poems* (1970), *Terms and Renewals* (1970), *Wild's Magical Book of Cranial Effusions* (1971), *Grace* (1972), *Peligros* (1972).

Miller Williams (born 1930 in Hoxie, Arkansas) is a poet, editor, teacher, critic, anthologist, and translator. He has edited *The Poems and Antipoems of Nicanor Parra* and *Chile: An Anthology of New Writing* and has written critical studies of the work of John Crowe Ransom and John Ciardi. Williams lives with his wife and three children in Fayetteville, Arkansas, where he teaches in the creative writing program of the University of Arkansas.

A Circle of Stone (1964), *Recital* (1965), *So Long at the Fair* (1968), *The Only World There Is* (1971).

William Carlos Williams (1883–1963) was born in Rutherford, New Jersey, where for most of his life he remained as a practicing pediatrician. While taking his M.D. degree at the University of Pennsylvania, he made friends with the poets Ezra Pound and H. D. (Hilda Doolittle). Surprisingly prolific for a busy doctor, Williams wrote, in addition to his poetry, fiction, plays, criticism, and essays in history (*In the American Grain,* 1939). His encouragement of younger poets, among them Allen Ginsberg, and the long-sustained example of his formally open poetry made him an appealing father-figure to the generation of Ginsberg, Gary Snyder, and Robert Creeley.

Collected Earlier Poems (1951), *Collected Later Poems* (1950), *The Desert Music* (1954), *Journey to Love* (1955), *Pictures from Brueghel* (1962), *Paterson* (collected edition, books 1 through 5, 1963), *Selected Poems* (1963).

Bruce P. Woodford (born 1919 in Astoria, Oregon) went to the University of Denver for three degrees, then taught at the University of Idaho. He is currently at Purdue.

Twenty-one Poems and a Play (1958), *Love and Other Weathers* (1966).

William Wordsworth (1770–1850) was born in England's Lake District, whose landscapes he was to embody in many of his poems. As a young man he visited France, sympathized with the Revolution, and met a young Frenchwoman, who bore him a child. In 1798 his friendship with Coleridge resulted in their publication of *Lyrical Ballads*, whose preface called for a poetry written "in the real language of men." Time brought him a quiet life, a small official job, a conventional marriage, a swing from left to right in his political sentiments, and appointment as poet laureate.

Poetical Works, ed. E. de Selincourt and Helen Darbishire (1940–1954), *The Prelude*, ed. E. de Selincourt (1928).

James Wright (born 1927 in Martins Ferry, Ohio) now lives in New York City and teaches at Hunter College. With Robert Bly, he has translated poems of César Vallejo, Pablo Neruda, and Georg Trakl. Since his first book, *A Green Wall* (1957), with its mastery of conventional forms, Wright has evolved a distinctive way of writing in open verse. In 1972 he received the Pulitzer Prize for poetry.

Collected Poems (1971).

Sir Thomas Wyatt (1503?–1542), English poet, diplomat, soldier, and courtier, twice saw the inside of prison when he slipped from the king's favor. Wyatt wrote remarkable love lyrics, among them the first sonnets in our language.

Collected Poems, ed. Kenneth Muir (1949), *Unpublished Poems by Sir Thomas Wyatt and His Circle*, ed. Kenneth Muir (1961).

William Butler Yeats (1865–1939) was born in Dublin, Ireland, the son of painter John Butler Yeats, and was irregularly schooled in Dublin and in London. Early in life Yeats sought to transform Irish folklore and legend into mellifluous poems and had he stopped in 1900 would be remembered as an outstanding minor Victorian. Instead, he became involved in the movement for an Irish nation (partly drawn into it out of his unrequited love for Maud Gonne, nationalist crusader and a great beauty) and in the founding of an Irish national theater. After the establishment of the Irish Free State, Yeats served as a senator. Partially because of the influence of Ezra Pound, his later poetry became harder and clearer. His lifelong interest in the occult culminated in his writing of *A Vision*, a document purportedly inspired by spirit masters.

Collected Poems (1956), *Collected Plays* (1952).

Al Young (born 1939 in Ocean Springs, Mississippi) attended the University of Michigan (where he edited the undergraduate magazine *Generation)* and Berkeley. He has worked as a professional musician and, besides his poetry, has written a novel, *Snakes*. At present he is Edward H. Jones Lecturer in Creative Writing at Stanford University.

Dancing (1970), *The Song Turning Back into Itself* (1971).

Paul Zimmer (born 1934 in Ohio) edits books for the University of Pittsburgh Press. In many of his recent poems, a character named Zimmer is central.

The Ribs of Death (1968), *The Republic of Many Voices* (1969).

Glossary of Terms
Possibly Useful for Discussing Poetry

Terms set in capital letters are defined elsewhere in the Glossary.

Accent. A greater amount of force given to one syllable than is given to another. For example, we stress the first syllable of *eagle, impact,* and *open,* and the second syllable of *cigar, precise,* and *until.*

Alliteration. A pattern of sound that occurs when the same consonant is repeated at the beginning of successive words: "Peter Piper picked a peck of pickled peppers." Alliteration may also occur within words — for example, the *k* sound in *picked, peck,* and *pickled* — in which case it is usually treated "internal alliteration."

Allusion. A reference to anyone or anything — fictitious, historical, actual. A poet who makes an allusion to Rip Van Winkle, to the Battle of Waterloo, or to Allen Ginsberg expects us to bring to an understanding of his poem some item of common knowledge.

Assonance. A pattern produced by the repetition of a vowel sound. Like alliteration, it may occur either initially (at the start of words) as in "all the awful auks" or internally (within words) as in the familiar phrase "holy smoke."

Ballad. A song or poem that tells a story. Some of the most famous ballads in English are folk ballads, loosely defined as anonymous story-songs transmitted orally before they were ever written down. Literary ballads are the work of poets consciously imitating folk or popular ballads.

Blank Verse. Lines written in unrimed IAMBIC PENTAMETER. This is the best-known one-line pattern for a poem in English. Most portions of Shakespeare's plays are in blank verse; so are Milton's *Paradise Lost* and certain dramatic poems of Tennyson, Browning, and Robert Frost. (Do not confuse blank verse with FREE VERSE.) Here is a poem in blank verse by John Keats that startles us by dropping out of its pattern in its final line:

> This living hand, now warm and capable
> Of earnest grasping, would, if it were cold
> And in the icy silence of the tomb,
> So haunt thy days and chill thy dreaming nights
> That thou wouldst wish thine own heart dry of blood
> So in my veins red life might stream again,
> And thou be conscience-calmed — see, here it is —
> I hold it towards you.

Carpe Diem. A Latin phrase meaning "seize today," passably well pronounced "carpa DEE-em." Poets ever since the Romans have used this familiar motif. Whenever a poet urges his lady to love him at once, without worrying about the future, because life is short, he is using the carpe diem theme. An example is Robert Herrick's "To the Virgins, to Make Much of Time": "Gather ye rosebuds while ye may."

371

Concrete Poetry. A movement widespread within the last ten years in which words are employed both for their meanings and for their appearances as graphic art. Most Concretists seem to make images or designs out of letters and words. In a famous example, the German poet-artist Reinhard Döhl constructed a silhouette shaped like an apple out of the word *apple* repeated seventy-nine times, with the word *worm* in the middle. An American Concretist, Mary Ellen Solt, has suggested that we can identify a Concrete poem by its "concentration upon the physical material from which the poem or text is made." Concrete poetry, then, appeals to the eye but is not necessarily representational.

Connotations. Associations or meanings that a word may suggest to a reader's mind, in addition to its denotation, or literal dictionary meaning. The word *skeleton*, for instance, denotes the bone-structure of a vertebrate animal, but its connotations may include thoughts of battlefields, ghosts in haunted castles, doctors' offices.

Couplet. A two-line STANZA, usually rimed. Its lines often tend to be of equal length, whether short or long.

Denotation. See CONNOTATIONS.

Dramatic Monologue. A poem cast as a speech by a single person, made at a decisive or revealing moment, usually addressed to another character, who does not speak.

Elegy. A poem whose TONE is melancholy or sadly contemplative, usually on the subject of death or the death of some person.

End-stopped Line. A line that ends in a full pause — usually indicated by a period, question mark, exclamation point, colon, or semi-colon. A line that ends with no punctuation, or with only a slight pause indicated by a comma, is called a "run-on" line.

Epigram. "A short poem ending in a witty or ingenious turn of thought, to which the rest of the composition is intended to lead up," according to the Oxford English Dictionary. (In prose, an epigram may be any terse, pointed statement.) An example from Alexander Pope, "Epigram Engraved on the Collar of a Dog":

> I am his Highness' dog at Kew;
> Pray tell me, sir, whose dog are you?

Feet. Units into which a metrical line can be divided; one of the molecules out of which a RHYTHM is made. In English, a foot usually consists of one stressed and one or two unstressed syllables. Two or more feet set in a line start a rhythm. The IAMB is the foot most commonly employed in English verse today; other feet, if set in a line for more than a couple of units, tend to sound artificial or even comic, as in Thomas Hood's "Bridge of Sighs," in which the metrical foot is the dactyl (one accented and two unaccented syllables):

> Make no deep scrutiny
> Into her mutiny . . .

Figure of Speech. A description of something in terms of something else. In general, a figure of speech may be said to occur when a speaker or writer departs from the usual denotations of words for the sake of freshness or emphasis. When Hamlet says he will "speak daggers," no one takes him literally. The figure of speech rests on the CONNOTATIONS of "daggers" — sharpness, stabbing, wounding — and their appropriateness to the way Hamlet spoke. Among the most common figures of speech are METAPHOR, SIMILE, PUN, and PERSONIFICATION.

Fixed Form. A familiar and agreed-upon pattern inherited from other poems — for example, the fixed form of the SONNET.

Free Verse. Poetry that does not consistently employ METER or RIME (from the French *vers libre*). No one seems happy with the expression, least of all the poets accused of being free versifiers, who (like William Carlos Williams) have protested that their work is anything but free and is guided and controlled by principles other than that of meter.

Heroic Couplet. Two rimed lines of IAMBIC PENTAMETER, the first ending in a light pause, the second more heavily END-STOPPED. It was much favored by English poets from about 1660 until the late eighteenth century. An instance from Samuel Johnson:

> Must helpless man, in ignorance sedate,
> Roll darkling down the torrent of his fate?

Iamb. A metrical foot consisting of one accented syllable followed by an unaccented syllable — for example, the word *indeed.*

Iambic Pentameter. A line consisting of five iambs. For a passage in iambic pentameter by Keats, see BLANK VERSE.

Image. A word or sequence of words that refers to any sensory experience. Though the term "image" suggests a thing seen, and though many images in poetry convey glimpses, an image may be an evocation of an odor, a taste, a sound, or a sensation such as pain, the pricking of gooseflesh, the quenching of thirst.

Incremental Refrain. See REFRAIN.

Literary Ballad. See BALLAD.

Lyric. As its Greek name suggests, a poem originally sung to the music of a lyre. Today, "lyric" usually denotes either the words to a song or a short poem expressing the thoughts and feelings of a speaker.

Metaphor. A figure of speech, a statement that one thing is something else, which (in a literal sense) it is not: "Life is a bowl of cherries." Metaphors in poetry are often not obviously indicated but are merely assumed or implied: "Life's ripe red fruit breaks men's teeth with its pits." In everyday speech we often use metaphors without being aware of them: "She's a doll." "What a swine he is!" Poets, however, invite us to be aware of metaphoric comparisons.

Metaphysical Poetry. A name applied to the work of John Donne and other poets who in mind and style resemble him. Metaphysical poets tend to convey subtle emotions and express spiritual relationships in startlingly physical terms: God's grace being compared to meat; the union of two lovers, to the bite of a flea. Often they delight in PUN and PARADOX.

Meter. The pattern of accented and unaccented syllables in a line of poetry. Meter is produced when stresses in a line recur at fixed intervals — for instance, as in IAMBIC PENTAMETER.

Neoclassical Poetry. Any poetry modeled after that of the ancient Greeks and Romans may be dubbed Neoclassical, but commonly the term refers to most English poetry written from about 1660 to 1780. Influenced especially by Latin precepts and practice, English poets favored a refined and decorous language of suitable loftiness (or lowliness, in the case of satire) and upheld standards of moderation and just proportion. Neatness of phrase was esteemed more highly than originality (true wit, according to Alexander Pope, being "What oft was thought but ne'er so well expressed"). SATIRIC POETRY was the favorite genre, the HEROIC COUPLET the favorite form, of Neoclassical poets.

Ode. In English poetry, a name usually applied to a lyric poem slightly longer than most lyrics and usually marked by a tone of seriousness and elevation (Wordsworth's "Ode: Intimations of Immortality," Shelley's "Ode to the West Wind").

Off-Rime. A rime in which the final consonant sounds are the same but the vowel sounds are different — for example, *flame* riming with *dim, lamb, gleam, doom,* and *glum.* Off-rime is also known as near-rime, half-rime, and slant-rime.

Onomatopoeia. The naming of a thing or action by a word or phrase that imitates the sound associated with it: *zoom, whiz, crash, bang, buzz, ding-dong, whoosh, pitter-patter, yakety-yak.*

Open Verse. Another name for FREE VERSE.

Paradox. A statement that seems self-contradictory but is not. "The peasant lives in a larger world than the globe-trotter," said G. K. Chesterton.

Paraphrase. To restate in one's own words what a poem seems to say.

Parody. A literary composition in which one writer pokes fun at another by imitating his style.

Pastoral. A genre of poetry dealing with shepherds and rural life, popular among the Romans and much imitated by English poets since the Renaissance. Pastoral poetry may portray the world of shepherds with some realism, as in Virgil's *Eclogues*, or it may make it a prettified Eden, as in Christopher Marlowe's "The Passionate Shepherd to His Love."

Personification. A figure of speech in which an object, an animal, or an abstraction (truth, nature) is presented as if it were human — for instance, Tennyson's image of an eagle, "He clasps the crag with crooked hands"; Keats's personification of fame as "a wayward girl."

Poetry. No definition exists to which there are no exceptions. Robert Frost wisely defined poetry as what poets write.

Projective Verse. A term used by the influential poet Charles Olson (1910–1970) to describe a kind of open verse in which the poet composes by listening to his own breathing and attempting to record it on the page by means of white space, indentations, and breaks in the middle of a line.

Prose Poem. A poem whose words are printed in a block like a paragraph, instead of being arranged in lines.

Pun. The use of words to suggest other words having the same or similar sound but a different denotation. For example, in *Romeo and Juliet*, as Mercutio dies he says: "Ask for me tomorrow, and you shall find me a *grave* man."

Quatrain. A stanza of four lines, usually rimed. The quatrain is the most frequently used STANZA in English verse.

Refrain. Words, phrases, or lines repeated at intervals in a song or songlike poem. A refrain usually follows immediately after a STANZA, and when it does, it is called a "terminal refrain." A refrain whose words change slightly every time they recur is called an "incremental refrain."

Rhythm. A movement marked by regular recurrences. A rhythm may inhere in the returns and departures of the seasons, in the repetition of a sound, in the beating of the heart. In poetry, when we speak of rhythm we generally mean not the repetition of a sound (as in RIME or ALLITERATION or ASSONANCE) but the recurrence of stresses and pauses with some regularity.

Rime. Defined most narrowly, rime (also spelled rhyme) occurs when two or more words or phrases contain an identical or similar vowel-sound, usually accented, and when the consonant-sounds (if any) that follow the vowel-sound are identical — *ripe* and *snipe*, *baloney* and *Maloney*, *prairie schooner* and *piano tuner*. From these examples it can be seen that rime depends not on spelling but on sound.

Rime Scheme. The order or sequence in which rimed words occur, customarily indicated by a convenient algebra. The rime scheme of this stanza is *a b a b*:

> Round, round, the roof doth run;
> And being ravished thus,
> Come, I will drink a tun
> To my Propertius.

Run-on Line. See END-STOPPED LINE.

Satiric Poetry. In a satiric poem, the poet ridicules people, or some aspect of human behavior, examining his victim by the light of his own principles and implying that the reader ought to join with him in mockery.

Scansion. An analysis of verse to determine its meter. Scansion reveals the stresses in a line or in a whole poem. Various marks can be used to indicate how heavily the syllables are accented. Here is a line scanned with ′ showing a stressed syllable and ‿ showing an unstressed syllable:

Ă búnch ŏf thĕ bóys wĕre whóop • ĭng ĭt úp ĭn the Mál • ă • mŭte să • lóon.

Sentimentality. The weakness of a writer who implies that he feels great emotion but fails to provide the reader with sufficient reason to feel it too. Tear-jerking verse about old locks of golden baby-hair and Grandmother's dear false teeth exhibit one kind of sentimentality. A popular songwriter who recently asserted that any driver who runs over a chipmunk on the highway deserves to go to Hell and have his eyes torn out exhibited another kind.

Simile. A figure of speech, a comparison of two things, indicated by a connective, usually *like, as, than,* or a verb such as *resembles.*

Sonnet. The fixed form that in English has attracted the largest number of practitioners. (The vogue for sonnets came over into Elizabethan England from Italy, in imitation of the sonnets of Petrarch.) The usual basic pattern of a sonnet is fourteen riming lines of iambic pentameter. In the English or Shakespearean sonnet the rimes are grouped into three quatrains and a final couplet. The Italian or Petrarchan sonnet avoids the final couplet. Its first eight lines (or octave) typically follow the rime scheme *a b b a a b b a;* in its last six lines (or sestet) the rime is *c d c d c d* or *c d e c d e* or some other variation that does not end in a couplet. No merely mechanical arrangement, the rime scheme of a successful sonnet embodies the structure of the poet's feelings and ideas. Accordingly, the English sonnet, with its couplet ending, tends to stop with a sort of epigram and lends itself to surprise conclusions. The Italian sonnet tends to divide, in its octave and sestet, into a statement of a problem or crisis and some manner of resolution.

Stanza. Italian for a "a room" or "a stopping-place." A stanza is a group of lines that usually has a pattern — a rime scheme, an arrangement of line-lengths — repeated throughout the poem. Songs fall into stanzas because musical passages are repeated and require the repetition of an arrangement

376

of words to fit them. When printed, the stanzas of songs and poems usually are set off from one another by space.

Stress. See ACCENT.

Subject. See THEME.

Surrealism. A movement in graphic art and poetry begun after World War I by the French poet and psychiatrist André Breton, who declared that there is a higher reality that to men's eyes would appear absurd. To mirror that reality, surrealist poets and artists have been fond of describing bizarre and dreamlike objects — fish that dissolve, white-haired revolvers.

Sutra. In Buddhism, a recorded dialogue of the Buddha, cast in poetic lines and sometimes intoned or chanted. In English, written recently by poets impressed by Eastern thought, sutras tend to be extended poems in open forms, expressing some personal illumination.

Syllabic Verse. A form of poetry, usually in stanzas, in which the poet devises a pattern of a certain number of syllables (not metrical feet) to a line and repeats it throughout the poem.

Symbol. In literature, a symbol is a verbal account of a visible object or action that suggests many meanings in addition to itself. A symbol does not "stand for" or "represent" any one meaning; it hints at infinite meanings. In Melville's novel *Moby Dick*, the great white whale is a symbol whose meanings may include the power of God, the indifference of the universe, the entire natural world. Thus Moby Dick reveals much more, with any thrash of his tail, than a whale could convey by himself.

Terminal Refrain. See REFRAIN.

Theme. The central thought conveyed by a poem. Theme is not the same as subject. A poem may have a rose for its subject-matter, but its theme may be, "Beautiful women soon wither and disappear, as roses do."

Tone. Like tone of voice, tone in poetry conveys an attitude — friendly or angry, sympathetic or aloof, earnest or playful. Usually when we ask, "What is the tone of a poem?" we mean, "What attitude does the poet take toward his theme or his subject?" Strictly speaking, tone is not the attitude itself— which may never be known for certain — but whatever in the poem makes an attitude clear.

Verse. Another name for poetry, any poetry. Verse is also a name for any composition in riming metrical lines, whether or not it is poetry:

> Roses are red,
> Violets are blue,
> Sugar is sweet
> And so are you.

This old jingle, which certainly rimes and scans, can hardly be called poetry. "Verse" is sometimes used to mean stanza: "Everybody join in and sing the second verse!"

377

The Poems and the Poets

381

6. The Image in the River: Peoples

7. The End of the World: Nightmare and Apocalypse

8. Pursuing the Horizon: Journeys

9. Strong Enchantments: Magic

384

10. Looking Down for Miles: Solitude

11. Eternal Summer: Loving

12. As Long as Forever Is: Enduring